Walk by My Side

A Solo Journey to Santiago on the Portuguese Camino

John Comando

INSIDE

"As I picked my way through [the rocks], suddenly, one of my walking poles slipped and I lurched to the left --- twisting my body, but breaking a fall.

Recovering my balance, I stopped and winced in pain. The suddenness of the mishap shook me. My thoughts were scrambled and, feeling out of control as adrenalin pumped through my body, a sense of panic swept over me.

It took a minute to gather myself as I stood, leaning on my poles, in the middle of "who knows where" and alone.

I remember thinking that this was a close call. If I had fallen, it could have been a lot worse. I could have twisted or dislocated my recently replaced right hip. I could have broken the hip or another limb. I felt lucky, but not too lucky. When I gathered my wits and started to walk again, the muscles on the left side of my back hurt at every step.

At the time, I couldn't have known that, whatever I had done to myself that morning, would affect the rest of my Camino, and I still had seven walking days to go to get to Santiago."

WALK BY MY SIDE

DEDICATION

This book is dedicated to Bonnie whose unwavering support helped me get through training, walking the Camino, and writing this book.

.

CONTENTS

ACKNOWLEDGMENTS

I never would have gone on a pilgrimage to Santiago without the inspiration from friends and acquaintances, including Patrick and Judy, Jim and Cathy, Connie and Linda. The stories of their Caminos educated me about what to expect and their advice was priceless.

Other friends gave me advice about and loaned me equipment for my trip, including Dennis, Calvin, and Hugh.

I received valuable feedback from several people who read early drafts of this book that led to major changes and ultimately a better book. They include, Marianna and Ken, Blue, Barbara, and Lawrence.

I read portions of the book at meetings of the Ajijic Writers Group in Mexico. Their comments highlighting the need to relate what I did and saw with what I thought and how I felt about it also helped produce a better book.

My editor, Sandi, encouraged me to pursue the spiritual development that evolved on my journey, and how my experiences changed the way I felt about the Camino.

All of this feedback transformed the book from a day-by-day travel journal to a travel memoir where I hope there's as much of me on its pages as there is the content of my journey.

Finally, I need to thank my girlfriend, Bonnie, who inspired the title, and was my biggest cheerleader.

My Camino Walk

PART 1

PREPARATION

1 DISCOVERING THE CAMINO

…"Someday I hope you get the chance
To live like you were dying
Like tomorrow was a gift
And you've got eternity
To think about
What you'd do with it
What could you do with it
What did I do with it?
What would I do with it?

From "Live Like You Were Dying"
Sung by Tim McGraw
Songwriters: Craig Michael Wiseman / James
Timothy Nichols / Tim Nichols

The soles of my feet were burning. It was the first weekend in August, and I was training to walk the Camino in Spain. At this hour, the sun beat down harshly on the small Mexican town where I live. I wished I hadn't left the bottle of water on a table at the plaza. Another 1.5 kilometers and my training walk for the day would be over. Parched and getting dehydrated, I stayed on the northern side of the Carretera where the broad arms of the trees overhanging the road offered more shade. Then, the trees disappeared, and it got more uncomfortable walking in full sun for half a kilometer, past the Tobolandia Waterpark, Walmart, and the stores and restaurants that lined the streets of San Antonio Tlayacápan.

I started this particular day at 7:00 am. The time on my cell phone registered almost 2:00. Today's walk was a dry-run, trying to complete 14 kilometers, about 9.4 miles, my longest training distance yet. On the Camino, I'd be walking close to 20 kilometers most days, so this walk would only get me to my shortest destination of 14 kilometers on the second day of my Camino. I reasoned that if I could complete 14 kilometers, I could tough out the rest on any given day.

Training had become an important part of my being. Every day I got up early to beat the blistering sun and walked…and walked with mind-numbing regularity. When I started, I was sorely out of shape and recovering from a hip replacement a year earlier. As my strength and stamina increased, so did my confidence. Regardless, I still had doubts.

When I started walking for exercise in the spring of 2018, I couldn't imagine walking the Camino de Santiago in Spain. But here I was, about to leave in a month to do it. Adventure beckoned, but I needed to answer some questions: Could I do it? Could I do the distance I planned to walk every day?

***

This book is about my Camino de Santiago pilgrimage at the ripe young age of seventy-one. The Camino is a pilgrimage that traditionally Catholics from all over the world undertake to the purported burial site of St. James at the cathedral in Santiago de Compostela, the capital of the Spanish autonomous region, Galicia. I say purported because there are historians who speculate that the person buried beneath the altar at the Cathedral might be someone else.

Regardless, in 1879, Pope Leo XIII officially declared the cathedral the burial site of St. James when a skull fragment from the remains in Santiago exactly matched a hole in the beheaded skull of St. James in Tuscany.

Santiago is the third most holy site in the Catholic religion after Jerusalem and Rome. And millions of people, including kings, queens, and popes have been making pilgrimages to it for centuries. There are numerous routes to the holy place. They follow age-old paths and modern highways from all over Europe. Most people only know about the Camino Frances which crosses the Pyrenees, and meanders across northern Spain for almost 800 kilometers (500 miles). In Spain alone, there are numerous others some of which are called the English, Northern, Primitivo, Portugues, and the Via de la Plata which stretches all the way from Seville in southern Spain.

A 2010 movie called "The Way," took place on the Camino Frances, and it inspired a new generation of pilgrims to make the trek. The Camino is no longer solely a religious endeavor. Participation on pilgrimages has mushroomed to hundreds of thousands of people every year.

About 42% of them claim to walk the Camino for religious reasons; 10% for no religious reason at all. The rest fall into a broad category that includes religious and "other" reasons.

I would put myself in the group that had no religious intent. While I experienced a certain spirituality, especially towards the end of my pilgrimage, I could never claim that I was actively seeking it when I started.

Having lived in the Boston area for more than forty years, the annual running of the Boston Marathon always fascinated me. At times, I even pondered running in it. But, in all my years, I never thought about walking the Camino de Santiago. After all, I'm not Catholic. As a matter of fact, I didn't know about it until a few years before.

When I started researching the Camino, I wasn't sure which of the many routes would be best for me given my age and physical condition. Eventually, I chose to walk the Camino Portugues, the second most walked pilgrimage route. It starts in Lisbon, and splits into the inland and coastal routes north of Porto. In its entirety, it is 616 kilometers (385 miles)

Because of my hip replacement, I specifically chose a 100 mile (160 km) segment of the coastal route, primarily because it had gentler elevations and seemed as though it would be easier. I planned a moderate pace averaging 10 to 12 miles a day, and built in two days of rest. The object was to get from point A to point B without killing myself. And, being retired, I had no time constraints on my adventure.

My route started in the seaside town of A Guarda at the Portuguese border with Spain and followed the Atlantic coast to the city of Vigo. From there, the coastal route heads inland. At a town called Redondela, the coastal route rejoins the inland route and proceeds to Santiago.

My Camino plans involved not just walking. I wanted my Camino experience to be about the things I discovered along the way. I walked close to the land, the people, the culture, and...the food. Part of my Camino experience included trying the different foods of the places I visited. What better way to learn about the areas I traversed than experiencing their gustatory delights.

However, the journey became more than the physical distance, terrain, and the places I visited. I started the journey with no particular reason for walking the Camino other than the challenge. The challenges that presented themselves on the way, however, transformed the experience in unexpected ways that I only realized near the end of my Camino.

This book is as much a travel narrative as it is a memoir of my Camino experience. It is not a "how-to" about how to plan and walk a Camino. Although, if you are planning to do one, you will find a lot of useful information related throughout the narrative. I didn't take many photos, but hope this book turns an old adage on its head. A picture can be worth a thousand words, but a thousand words can express so much more than any picture can. This book is about what *I* experienced.

So join me now and walk by my side as we start our journey from Mexico to Santiago.

2 RAMBLIN' FEVER

Ramblin' fever
The kind that can't be measured by degrees
Ramblin' fever
There ain't no kind of cure for my disease

Songwriter: Merle Haggard Ramblin' Fever lyrics
© Sony/ATV Music Publishing LLC

In May 2017, I was staying in a suburb of Boston, Massachusetts, recovering from a hip replacement. The physical therapist told me I was making great progress. I could now take myself for unassisted walks using crutches. As I maneuvered the crutches down the sidewalk one crisp afternoon, I couldn't help notice that spring bloomed all around me. Trees filled with young green leaves, and buds popped out in every direction. The light breeze carried their sweet scents my way.

During those days, I could never imagine that less than a year and a half later I would walk a challenging 100 miles on the Camino Portugues. Back then, I didn't even know about the Camino de Santiago, let alone a Portuguese Camino.

Who knows, maybe I was destined to walk the Camino. From the time I turned ten years old, when my parents put me on a plane to visit a friend on Cape Cod, I've always had wanderlust. My parents continued to cultivate my interest in travel by often putting me on a bus and sending me to visit my grandmother in Pennsylvania. I appreciated every chance I could get to travel. By the time I got to high school, I had ridden trains from New Jersey to Colorado and New Mexico, as well as northern Wisconsin. Travel had me hooked.

Back in the early 1960s, I was unusual among my group of friends. They preferred to stay closer to home. During summer vacations, we rode our bikes everywhere. Jockey Hollow National Battleground in Morristown, NJ, about 10 miles away, was about as far afield as we would go. On those hot summer days we almost always stopped at Welsh's Ice Cream on the way home. It happened that on one of these days, in the shade of a tall oak, that I popped the question.

"Would any of you guys be interested in riding our bikes across the country," I tentatively questioned. I had read about someone our age doing it, and had already researched it.

"You mean to California?" One of the guys asked. "Yeah," I answered. Then the laughing started. They didn't want to hear about my research. "What a hare-brained idea," one of my friends said.

I figured that if I wanted to ride my bike across the country, I would have to do it alone.

Well, I never did it. But almost every time I get together with a group of my buddies, someone brings it up, and they all have a laugh on me.

I wound up going to college halfway across the country in Michigan. That required taking buses, trains, and airplanes -- until I got a car. That enabled me to explore the countryside further. My college sent me abroad to Spain to study in my junior year. Like most students who have that experience, I used my vacations while there to travel all over Europe.

Since then, my travels have taken me on a road trip across Canada, all over Latin America, where I adopted two children and built houses for Habitat for Humanity, and to a retirement in the central highlands of Mexico.

I retired to the Lake Chapala region of Mexico in 2014. Lake Chapala is the largest lake in Mexico and is located only an hour south of Guadalajara, Mexico's second largest city. The climate there is like spring time most of the year.

My plan, when I moved to Mexico, included using the savings from living there to travel. So, after four years of only traveling back to the U.S. and the Pacific Ocean beaches, I was getting bored. If there isn't any focus or purpose to your life, retirement can make you complacent. It was time to shake things up; time to start executing my original plan. Having lived in Spain as a student 50 years earlier, a return visit there sat high on my agenda.

There's a big retired population living on the north shore of the lake. Several friends who had completed a Camino introduced me to what I would call the Camino "phenomenon." Their stories piqued my interest.

I had started walking for exercise in spring, 2018. When I walked for long periods of time, I thought of all sorts of things. At some point, during my "exercise walks," my thoughts turned to planning a trip to Spain. Then, after hearing stories of other people's Caminos, I got another hare-brained idea of combining my trip with a Camino experience.

So, given my history and penchant for wanderlust, when I told people I planned to walk a hundred miles in Spain, most of the people I knew were un-phased. The most often asked question I got was, why?

My thoughts were, why not?

3 POSSIBILITIES

When I returned to my home in Mexico after my surgery, walking for exercise and therapy became part of my daily routine. I didn't walk far. Despite excellent mobility, my hip hadn't healed completely. I didn't want to put undue strain on it. But, if I lost a few pounds in the process of walking, I reasoned, it would put less stress on the hip and help it heal.

Attitude became the biggest hurdle in continuing to walk on a consistent basis. You see, I hate exercise. However, I'm very goal oriented. Process is fine, but I need a product at the end. Walking for walking's sake, doesn't cut it. I need a goal to be walking toward. That goal eventually became the Camino.

Around the same time I started my walking regimen in early spring 2018, I started to learn about the Camino. One evening my girlfriend and I had dinner with a couple, Patrick and Judy, who were planning to walk it. It seemed like such a way-out thing to do at the time. They were planning to walk the Camino Frances from St. Jean de Pied in France, over the Pyrenees, and across northern Spain for 800 kilometers (500 miles). That idea seemed crazy for someone my age and in my physical condition. It would take them more than a month, and they would need to carry everything on their back. As they spoke about their plans, I could see their excitement. The challenge began to interest me.

I filed the challenge in the back of my mind. However, it kept popping out during my early morning walks when anything and everything seemed to pop into my head. Then a few weeks later, after Patrick and Judy had left for their pilgrimage, I inquired of the whereabouts of a friend, Linda, whom I hadn't seen for a long time. Her friend informed me that she was walking the Camino in Spain. "*What a strange coincidence*," I thought, that three people I knew had taken up the challenge at the same time.

Later, in a casual conversation with a world-traveling friend, Connie, I learned that she had walked part of the Camino Frances the autumn before. In the spring, I ran into another couple, Jim and Kathy, who had just returned after shadowing the trip of Patrick and Judy. For months, I kept uncovering more people who had, at one time or other, completed the walk to Santiago.

What was going on here? Was this a trend? I'm not a trendsetter and rarely a trend follower. I like to think that I march to my own beat. However, as I walked every day, the idea of walking a Camino continued to go through my mind.

I started researching the Camino and found that there

was more than one. I learned that one started in Portugal, a place I wanted to visit. So, I looked further and found out that part of the Camino Portugues followed the coast. That meant that it would be relatively flat. I could walk a good portion of the Camino under conditions similar to those in my area of Mexico – albeit at 5,000 feet lower altitude.

What better way to walk the Camino than by the sea. I love the ocean. I could spend all day looking at it; listening to waves crashing on the shore; and smelling its brininess in the breeze. Except for six years, I never lived more than an hour from the ocean. There's something rejuvenating about walking along the surf, while lost in thoughts that I never get tired of. When I lived in Massachusetts, I would get up with the sun and drive 45 minutes to Duxbury Beach where I would walk alone for more than an hour, and be gone long before the first sunbather arrived.

During my research, I also found out that I didn't have to walk the entire route. I could walk part of it to qualify as a pilgrim. Sixty miles (100 kilometers) enabled one to qualify, not 500 like some of my friends had done. And, I didn't need to carry a pack either. There were services that would do it for me.

Walking the Camino started to become more and more possible.

4 TRAINING, SHOPPING, AND PLANNING

Training for the Camino became all about getting to know my body, especially legs and feet, and understanding which equipment worked well.

When I started walking, I wore an old pair of sneakers that weren't good walking shoes, at least not the kind of walking I planned to do. Walking every day, it didn't take long before the sneakers started to fail, as well as my feet. Once I made the decision to walk the Camino, I quickly realized that I needed to buy appropriate footwear.

Now, there are many opinions on the proper footwear. Walking the part of the Camino Portugues that I'd be walking for 12 days did not require a rugged pair of hiking boots. They would need an extensive amount of time to break in, and would add unnecessary weight. I tried a casual walking shoe but it didn't fit properly in the toes, and after a few morning walks, I put them on a shelf, never to be worn again. I quickly learned that my wide feet would need plenty of toe room.

Then one afternoon, while talking with a friend, Dennis, at a local bar, about needing sneakers for walking, he started to rave about the sneakers he wore, Saucony Trek 11. He had brought them from the states. Calvin, the bartender chimed in that he wore them too, and said that despite being on his feet all day, they were incredibly comfortable. The Trek line is a hiking/trail sneaker. It has a good tread, decent arch support, and the sizes tend to run wide. I decided to give them a try.

However, I had a small problem. Saucony shoes are difficult to find in this part of Mexico. Not many retailers sell them. Amazon won't ship them to Mexico, and since sneaker brands tend to be sized differently, I didn't know the correct size to order. This would require a trip to the big city, Guadalajara. By this time, I had made lists of the equipment I needed to buy and could find there.

I had to visit two large shopping malls in Guadalajara before I could find the Saucony sneakers. The chain sporting goods store had none in my normal size. However, I tried a pair two sizes larger. They fit my wide foot well except for the toes. I bought them and a wicking athletic shirt. Then I visited an outdoors sports outfitter where I found more equipment that I needed.

The first time I wore the sneakers, my toes swam in them. The extra room would come in handy after walking a while, but I needed to make adjustments. So I added a fiber-like material insole to make the sneakers fit tighter and keep my toes from moving. In addition, my friend

Linda, who had been afflicted with shin splints and blisters during her pilgrimage, suggested gel-soles. She, along with everything I read, reiterated the importance of foot care.

Over the summer, several foot problems arose, and I experimented with different types of supports to solve them. My sneakers had gel-soles on the bottom and extra arch support. I taped my heel every day with surgical tape to prevent blisters, and I wore a pressure ankle brace because my ankles got sore. I'm not sure if I needed all these fixes because my sneakers didn't fit correctly, but I trained all summer and walked 100 miles relatively problem-free.

One of the things I would need was a backpack. So, I started looking online, and at Walmart and other local stores without luck or knowing what to buy. I told myself that this also might require a trip to Guadalajara. But then I got lucky. One of the places I would walk on a regular basis was the town of Chapala, three miles down the carretera. Often, I would meet a friend of mine, Hugh, for coffee before returning home. I told him about my plans, and he immediately offered me a backpack he had used to travel around Central America. His 48 liter Ozark Mountain pack with a built in frame and lots of compartments and adjustments for comfort would be perfect.

A lot of the stuff I needed I found online, including walking poles and a Tilly Hat. I look funny in my Tilly, but I wanted a flexible, waterproof hat with a wide brim that could cover the back, south-facing, part of my neck. I think I look strange in my Tilly, and affectionately refer to it as my "Dork" hat.

I was undecided whether I should take walking poles until the last week before leaving. I had never used them before. In retrospect, I'm glad I had them. They became invaluable when walking down steep grades, especially when fatigue set in and I experienced pressure on my leg muscles and hip.

As the summer of 2018 raced along, I became more and more invested in walking the Camino. I had bought equipment and airplane tickets, reserved accommodations, and had planned four weeks of travel with my girlfriend in Portugal and Spain after completing the Camino. All my friends knew about this extensive trip, including the Camino.

There were times that summer, training in the hot sun, that I questioned why I should tackle such a challenge. I could just chuck it, travel around Spain and Portugal, and avoid all the pain. But I did have a major problem. I had told so many people, that it would be an embarrassment to quit. Besides, I'm not a quitter. When I commit to something, I follow through.

On September 10, my girlfriend and I packed up my 2006 Toyota Camry, and drove north. After dropping her at her daughter's house in New York State, I continued to Boston where I visited with my kids, sold the car, and got on a plane to Porto, in Portugal.

5 AIRPLANES, SUBWAYS, AND BUSSES

"So… this is it," I said to myself as I surveyed the hotel room to make sure I hadn't left anything. I arrived in Porto, Portugal, the day before and it was day-one of the trip I had been planning for months.

I lifted my knapsack up on my shoulders, and grabbed my daypack off the bed. Taking a last look at the room, I closed the door and turned to walk down the three flights of stairs to the street. I dropped the key at the desk on my way down at 7:30.

I needed to catch an 8:45 bus to the border with Spain. I wasn't sure how long it would take to get to the bus station and what to expect when I got there. I needed to travel half-way across Porto and would be taking the Metro. So I gave myself plenty of time.

Stepping out onto the carless street, I felt a brief chill. The previous day, sizzling temperatures of more than 90 degrees Fahrenheit seared the city. But, it being the end of September, I wished I had dressed for the cool morning temperature.

My feet and legs felt ready as I started down the hill retracing my steps from the day before to the Bolhao

Metro Station. I turned right onto an empty Rua Santa Caterina, a pedestrian shopping street that, in a short while, would be teeming with people. I trudged up the two blocks where I'd catch the subway.

All over Porto, there were scores of people taking the first steps of their Camino just like me. They might be walking to Rua de Cedofeita and the continuation north of the Central route of the Camino Portugues. Or they might start the Coastal route near the cathedral and walk west along the Duoro River to the Atlantic Ocean and then north. Some might hop on the same Metro as me and take a shortcut to Matesinhos on the Atlantic where the Coastal route passes.

I needed to take the Metro just three stops to Casa de Musica bus station where I'd catch a bus to the border.

The people of Porto seemed to be indifferent to the thousands of pilgrims, or *peregrinos*, who invade their city each year. Back packs and walking poles don't raise an eyebrow on the city's busy streets. As I walked to the subway, waited on the platform, and stepped onto the train, no one gave me a second look.

After leaving the train, a welcomed escalator carried me to the street corner across from the Casa de Musica station. It was a non-descript structure that served as an open-air shelter for commuters who queued up for their busses. I didn't see any ticket office – only a small café doing a brisk business selling coffee and pastries. Fortunately, I had purchased my ticket online.

The bus didn't leave for a half hour. Several ambivalent

Russian travelers stood around trying to figure out where the ALSA bus to Spain would board. They spoke English to me, and told me that they were on vacation for a few weeks and on their way to Santiago. After asking a few questions, a passerby assured us of the correct location.

My first, most important, cup of coffee and breakfast beckoned me from the cafe. I stepped up to the counter and ordered Café Americano and a croissant. Sitting at a plastic table, I waited for the bus's arrival. I watched the commuters, and wondered about a sports team, that sat at two tables near me and where they were going with their duffle bags.

A column of steam rose from the cup as it warmed my hands. I started pulling the croissant apart, unraveling its rolls by pulling the pastry apart at the center. Portuguese croissants are cakey and sweet, not crispy and flakey like the French version. The coffee smelled strong and aromatic and tasted satisfying. I ordered a second cup.

The bus pulled in right on time. I threw my backpack in with the suitcases and hopped on board. While the bus went all the way to Santiago de Compostela, I'd be getting off at the border town called Tui. There, I'd catch another bus to the starting point of my Camino on the coast.

ALSA is a pretty big international bus line in Europe. It's sort of like the Greyhound of Europe in more ways than one. I hoped that ALSA would be a step up from what US bus travelers have come to expect. You see, I live in Mexico where intercity bus travel is close to luxurious compared to what I found on ALSA. Squeezing into my seat, I immediately noticed no video screen on the seatback in front of me, or free snack, Wi-Fi, or even a restroom. Like in olden days, the bus had a rest stop so the driver and passengers could avail themselves of such services.

The group of Russians took the front seats and the sports team sat near the back. I sat alone, happy to be by myself. It was too early to carry on a conversation, so I welcomed the empty seat next to me, relieved that I wouldn't need to talk with anyone and could relax before confronting the unknown once more.

As the bus plied the streets of Porto on its way to the expressway, I settled back, and watched the scenery pass outside the window. We drove north through an endless maze of interchanges and toll booths and into the heart of northern Portugal. Multi-family homes and apartment buildings dotted undulating hills.

The Portugal that raced past the bus' window looked like a suburban country until we were past the rest stop at Braga. There, the hills became wooded and rural, demarcated by small towns and farms with their rock walls and fences. Foliage season had already started in New England where I had once lived. Despite being at about the same latitude, Portugal was still green. The corn stalks were yellow, but the only leaves turning colors were the grape leaves that remained in the vineyards after harvest.

6 CREDENCIALES, CACHORRINHOS, & FRANCESINHAS

The bus trip gave me three hours to reflect on my journey so far. I had been in mainland Portugal for less than 24 hours. Flying in from Boston on Azores Airlines, I had technically entered Portugal and the European Union somewhere in the middle of the Atlantic Ocean, Punta Delgado, where I changed planes. Once in Porto, a taxi strike greeted me and added confusion to my arrival. I hadn't made alternative arrangements or hired a driver, and would need to take the Metro downtown.

My walk on the Camino would be the first stage of a three stage trip to Portugal and Spain over several months. The temperature in Porto that day registered 90 degrees F, and I carried way too much luggage for my liking, especially in the heat.

Three pieces of luggage weighed me down, and the thought of maneuvering this load through the throngs of people jostling to purchase tickets appeared daunting. The lines to buy tickets were long at the machines in the Metro station, and the process was confusing for a foreigner without knowledge of Portuguese. Luckily a young woman who spoke English helped me navigate the system.

As I entered the jammed Metro car, there was little room to spare. The passengers stood squeezed shoulder to shoulder. The crowd hardly offered enough room to stand with my luggage. Despite air conditioning, it felt very hot and the discomfort registered strongly on passenger faces.

I got off the Metro downtown and lugged two suitcases and a day pack from the Bolhao Metro stop to my hotel. Three flights of steep stairs to my room confronted me. I wasn't expecting this surprise. Because of my hip and the steepness of the stairs, I dragged each bag separately hoping not to aggravate my hip. It didn't go well. At one point I wrenched my hip and felt a sharp pain while maneuvering the larger suitcase up a step.

"*Great*," I said to myself, standing as if suspended halfway up the first flight and wondering what my next move should be. "*What a way to start the trip…with a sore hip!*"

At least I had 36 hours until I started my walk. It was plenty of time, I hoped, for ibuprofen to do its magic.

When I got to the room, it was a basic space with a comfortable bed, tiny bathroom, and a working air conditioner. I immediately dug into my carry-on bag to find an ibuprofen.

I had devised an ingenious way to pack for my three month trip. My bags were like Russian nesting dolls. The large bag contained items that I wouldn't need until the last part of my trip, but with lots of extra room. My carry-on had most of my post Camino clothes. For the plane, I packed the backpack I'd use on the Camino in the large suitcase. Once in Porto, I removed the backpack and replaced it with the carry-on. I would be storing the large suitcase with the carry-on inside while I walked.

Because of the taxi strike, I needed to lug my big bag a half-hour across hilly Porto to where I dropped it at a luggage storage place. This left me with just my backpack and day pack to bring on the Camino. The backpack carried everything I would need, and then-some, for my twelve day trek. I would use a third party luggage livery service to carry it from hotel to hotel. That would enable me to walk with a small, light-weight, daypack containing water and a few essentials like first-aid stuff, a rain poncho, and my tablet, which I didn't want to entrust to a third party.

Every pilgrim carries a *"Credencial del Peregrino."* It's like a passport booklet that the pilgrim has stamped at various locations along the Camino such as hotels, hostels, restaurants, and stores. Many of the businesses offer discounts or special meals to pilgrims. The *credencial* provides proof that you are a pilgrim, but also that you have traversed the required distance to Santiago de Compostela. A pilgrim needs to walk at least 100 kilometers (60 miles) -- and prove it -- to receive a *compostela*, a certificate of achievement. I calculated my walk to be 160 kilometers (100 miles).

I needed to find the cathedral to acquire a credencial. You would think that the cathedral would be easy to find. From the luggage drop-off, it wasn't. So, after, dropping off my bags, I wandered around, unable to make sense of my tourist map, asking directions at every other corner until I found the cathedral. There, I purchased my credencial for 2 Euros, and had it officially stamped. I was now an official pilgrim!

Because of my exhaustion from the heat, being jet-lagged, and feeling numb from weariness, the moment seemed anti-climactic. Getting the credencial had been just another task I could check-off of my to-do list. Now that I had completed all my tasks for the day, I badly needed a cold beverage. I didn't have far to go. I came upon a sidewalk café a block away from the Cathedral on a street busy with tourists. I found an empty table in the welcoming shade facing down the hill to the Luiz 1 Bridge. Two glasses of chilled white wine later, I was fortified and ready to head back to my hotel for a nap.

Using my tourist map for "guidance," I took the back streets, and stumbled upon one of the "attractions" I wanted to experience in Porto, *Cervejeria Gazela*, home of the original *cachorrinho*. *Cachorrinhos* are a local food specialty. They consist of a long Portuguese spiced hot dog in an appropriately long roll with cheese and sauce. They are then pressed, cut into bite-size pieces and served with French fries and beer. It sounds very regular, but the flavor, like many other local delicacies, is more than the sum of its parts.

Anthony Boudain's documentary, *Parts Unknown*, talked

about the food in Porto and highlighted the *cachorrinho* in one segment. I had made a note to try one when I got to town. So, I sat at the bar, ordered a *cachorrinho* and a beer and asked the waiter if this was *the* famous place. He replied in the affirmative and showed me a picture on the wall of Bourdain with the owner to prove it! By chance, I had found the very establishment featured in the show.

Cachorrinho is the poor cousin of another local favorite food, the *Francesinha*. Waddling back to my hotel, I noticed that two of the top-rated restaurants in Porto known for their *Francesinhas* were just steps away from my hotel door. You can find this multi-layered sandwich all over Porto. Typically, it is made of two thick square pieces of brioche-type bread that's layered with several cheeses and meats. It's pressed, then cheese is melted over it, and it's dressed with a tomato sauce, as well as an optional fried egg, and a side of fries.

Not a bad sandwich for 8-12 Euros. It's enough calories for two days of walking the Camino. Needless to say, I fortified myself with one before bedtime.

7 WELCOME TO GALICIA

After three hours, the ALSA bus stopped to let me off at a gas station/convenience store on a corner at the southern edge of Tui. After climbing off, I collected my knapsack from the hold. With a "pssss" of the airbrakes, the door shut and the bus nudged its way back onto the street.

"*Now what?*" I said to myself, as I stood there with cars behind me queuing up for gas. I had made it to Spain, but in Tui, twenty five miles up the Minho River from A Guarda, my destination. The bus to A Guarda ran every hour, and it was scheduled to arrive in about 20 minutes. A little concerned, I had no clue where to meet it.

Being able to speak Spanish, I knew I could make myself understood. So, I went into the convenience store and found that the bus stopped right across the street. Moving my stuff, I set up watch. The blue and white ATSA (that's not a typo) bus appeared coming my way. After flagging it down, the driver stopped and with a hissing sound, the jaw-like door to the luggage compartment opened. I threw my pack in the cavernous, empty space, and climbed on. With more leg room and newer seats, this local bus was more comfortable than the international one.

The bus headed down highway N-551 following the route of the out-of-view Minho River. Vineyards, wineries and small towns lined the highway. This was the O Rosal sub region of the Rias Baixas winegrowing area that is famous for its crisp and fruity Albariño white wines. I'd have to wait for lunch to taste any.

A Guarda sits at the southwest corner of Galicia. The Minho River flanks it to the south and the Atlantic Ocean to the west. Sta. Tecla Mountain, on a peninsula to the south, commands a view of the mouth of the Minho.

Rolling into A Guarda, the bus stopped to discharge passengers at Parque Alameda, an unassuming patch of green. I recognized it from Google Street View. It seemed like I had "walked" from here to my hotel, Hotel Bruselas, before, and arrived in about five minutes without getting lost.

Hotel Bruselas had a small reception area and a good size bar/restaurant where about a dozen locals drank beer and watched a futbol game.

The manager was waiting for my arrival and greeted me in English. He inquired whether I was walking the Camino, then told me the hotel served breakfast at 8:00 am. He assumed I'd be leaving earlier, and asked me if I would like a snack for the road in lieu of the breakfast.

Accepting his offer, we proceeded with check-in. As he led me to the elevator, he reminded me to pick-up the snack around 8:30 that evening.

My bright, sunny and modern room sat on the west-facing corner of the third floor. I dropped my stuff and took a few bounces on the bed. It was more comfortable than the night before, and would be more than adequate.

My stomach needed some serious attention. It was after 1:00 pm and I hadn't eaten anything since Porto at 8:30.

Before my trip, I had researched A Guarda, and its restaurants. Seafood is the specialty. I had spent the previous day gorging myself on pork and beef products, so I felt excited to try the region's seafood. A Guarda is a fishing village that supplies the rest of Galicia and Spain with fish of all types. It is also a popular summer and weekend tourist destination for people living in the city of Vigo, a three day hike for me further up the road. My online search had yielded a list of three restaurants to try for seafood. The menus and photos intrigued me, and all of them were on a street that lined the harbor, and would be easy to find.

At the front desk, I asked for directions to the harbor. One block from the hotel, I made a wrong turn and found myself on a street heading south out of town.

8 FIRST TASTES OF SPAIN

Luckily, I could see the harbor to my right down a steep hill. Choosing a promising looking street, I turned right. The narrow street could hardly accommodate a car and pedestrian at the same time. It was lined with two and three story stone-faced homes that looked like they had been there for a century or more. The street zigged and zagged until it ended at a roundabout at the opposite end of the harbor from where I should have been.

On the other side of the roundabout I saw a building that looked like it could be the fish pier and market. A breakwater extended beyond the building forming a bowl-shaped harbor and safe haven for fisherman. The town rose on a hill opposite the breakwater. A semi-circular esplanade lined with restaurants and bars hugged the shore

I imagined a postcard-perfect Sunday in August with the esplanade filled with people sitting under a sea of multi-colored umbrellas enjoying glasses of wine and beer. But, on this Wednesday at the end of September, the vacationers and weekenders had gone home. The esplanade appeared abandoned except for some locals and me looking for a meal.

I strolled down the street, breathing in the fresh, salty sea air, and feeling a chill from a gentle breeze as I walked in the shadows formed by the buildings and the hill behind them. I began looking for those three restaurants on my list, but with disappointment found that two were closed, and the menu of the third didn't appeal to me. So, I started back to the roundabout where I had passed a relatively full restaurant, called Trasmallo. It offered a 15 Euro "Menu del Dia."

It's my understanding that when Franco ruled Spain, he mandated that every restaurant must offer a reasonably priced mid-day meal for the working people. It has become an institution all over the Iberian Peninsula, including Portugal. Today, the menu del dia typically includes two courses, dessert, and beverage (often including wine or beer). Trasmallo's menu looked good, so I decided to give it a try.

The restaurant had two dining rooms. You entered into a dark room with an open kitchen at the opposite end. There were fish tanks filled with the bounty of the sea. The people sitting at the tables appeared to be locals. To the right of the entrance were stairs leading to a bright and almost filled dining room that overlooked the harbor. I climbed up the stairs to the dining room and a waiter seated me at one of the two available tables.

Most of the people appeared to be vacationers. A van full of English-speaking tourists in hiking garb on a day trip from Santiago sat at one table. There were couples from Spain and others speaking languages I couldn't identify. Sumptuous plates of cured Spanish ham, calamari, steamed mussels, clams, and shellfish of all sorts, including lobster and crabs filled the tables of the hungry lunch crowd.

The waiter handed me a menu that did not include the menu del dia. So, I asked him for one. He hesitated for a second as if not sure what to do. "Of course, senor," he answered me, and went to consult with another waiter. It was becoming obvious to me, that few, if any people ordered the menu del dia in *this* dining room. They were probably relegated to the dark room below.

Nevertheless, the waiter graciously handed me "the menu," and I ordered a glass of the white house wine before he could leave. I started with an *ensalada rusa* for my first course. It turned out to be a Gallician potato salad, and was disappointing. But the *Merluza*, Hake, that I had for the second course, tasted like it had been caught that morning or plucked from one of the fish tanks downstairs just for me, and cooked to perfection. It turned out to be a wonderful meal, despite my chilly welcome.

***

Quite sated, I headed across the esplanade toward the center of town to walk off my meal. I decided to explore A Guarda's winding streets to find the Camino route for the next morning. I needed to find a church, which is a landmark where the route passes. I climbed a steep incline up from the harbor on cobblestone streets. I had read that the Camino in this part of town is not well marked, and I would need to find my way in the dark the next morning.

Most of the time, yellow arrows and seashells mark the Camino way and point the direction to Santiago. You can find yellow arrows painted on streets, buildings, poles, trees, and rocks. The seashells, while also painted on structures can also be found engraved and painted on granite markers sunk in the ground. The markers also show the distance left to walk to Santiago via the Camino.

An *albergue* sat just around the corner from the church. It abutted the highway, but also sat on the Camino route, and would be much easier to find in the dark. Rather than navigate the winding streets in the dark, I decided to start there.

Feeling confident, I headed down the main street and back to the hotel for a nap.

***

After my nap, I went out to explore a little further. This time, I took the correct turn which put me on a narrow shopping street. The sun was fading in the sky, and the shops had recently re-opened after their mid-day break. The entire street looked to be enshrouded in shadows. I proceeded down the gentle slope, stopped at a cell phone store and purchased a Spanish SIM card for my cell phone. Continuing, I found myself at the harbor. The hour was a little early for dinner and a little too soon after lunch. But because I would be rising early in the morning, I decided it would be best to find a snack now – maybe a few tapas - so I wouldn't be retiring on a full stomach. Once more, I started checking out the restaurants in the harbor area. I stopped at Cervejeria Celtic where about 10 people sat at various tables under an unassuming enclosed canopy. Cervejaria Celtic doesn't sound very Spanish, but centuries ago the Celts had a lot of influence in the region that you can still see today.

The tapas menu on the board outside looked interesting and the prices reasonable. I sat at a table facing the harbor. Two business men, deep in conversation, sat at one table smoking. At another table a couple sat across from each other holding hands. Several families sat on a stone wall, along the esplanade, drinking beer and watching the sun sink into the sky. When their beers were empty, one of them would return it to the Celtic and leave with another.

When the middle-aged waitress, dressed in black, arrived, I ordered a local Albariño and asked for a menu. The cool, crisp white wine accompanied me as I perused the restaurant's tapas offerings. I settled on steamed mussels and Padron peppers. But, when the food arrived, massive portions heaped in serving bowls, my first thought was, *"How am I going to eat all this?"* But me being me, I knew that some way, somehow, I would find a way!

I later found out that there are three ways to order tapas: as a snack, half-portion, or full portion. I'm not sure which size I ordered, but it seemed to be definitely more than a snack.

For a nothing little place, the food surprised me. The mussels were large and plump with bright orange bellies. They tasted succulent and sweet, bursting with the flavor of the sea and white wine. I think these were the sweetest mussels I've ever eaten – even sweeter than when I would pick them off the rocks in New England. Then there came the Padron peppers. They are green and about the size of a small jalapeño pepper, but carry none of the fiery kick. The Spanish sauté them in olive until the skin blisters and serve them in a simple way sprinkled with sea salt. You eat them by holding the stem and biting off the fruit. It's a great way to eat your vegetables.

***

Back at the hotel, I picked up my snack for the next day, and retired for the night wondering what adventures would come my way in the morning.

PART 2

LAUNCH

9 SOMEWHERE BEYOND THE SEA

I seem to have this recurring neurotic drama when I'm closing a door behind me and there's no going back. Every morning during my Camino I would go through the same doubts in my mind: Do I have everything? Did I check this or that? Should I go to the bathroom one more time? Will the livery service find my knapsack? Will it be safe? Do I need another layer of clothing?

I would stand there with the door cracked open asking myself until I had satisfactorily met all the conditions of departure. Because, at most of the places I stayed, I left before anyone else, and when the latch clicked shut, I couldn't get back in for at least an hour.

So there I stood in the doorway of the Hotel Bruselas with the door handle in my left hand and walking poles in my right. I had placed my pack behind the desk, trusting that Tuitrans, the service I engaged to move my backpack from hotel to hotel, would be by shortly to pick it up. Pre-dawn darkness loomed and the air felt crisp. Mustering my will, I snapped the door shut and facing the street started walking toward the highway and the *albergue.*

Finally, I was walking the Camino! No going back!

After three blocks, Cafeteria Oasis stood on the corner at the highway, with its lights bright against the darkness, welcoming customers for business. I hadn't had any coffee yet, so I sat at the counter and ordered what would become my Camino early morning breakfast, a café Americano and croissant.

One of the things I noticed is that the Spanish still read newspapers. Every bar has a selection. There were about half a dozen people sipping their coffees and reading newspapers. A news reader on the television over the bar also babbled the morning's news and weather in rapid-fire Spanish. I sat and savored the morning's first jolt of java. But I felt anxious and a need to get going.

Today, September 26, marked the first day of my Camino, and the culmination of months of training. I'd be walking from A Guarda to a small village, Viladesuso, a distance of about 16.7 kilometers (10 miles). The Camino follows Highway 552 up the coast, paralleling the Atlantic Ocean. Highway 552 has a bike path on the southbound side, and the Camino proceeds weaving its way from coastal paths to the bike path and back.

I hiked the half kilometer up the highway from the café to the municipal albergue at the top of a gentle hill. At 7:30, the *albergue* buzzed with activity. Pilgrims were preparing and eating breakfast or making last minute adjustments to their equipment. Some sat outside smoking cigarettes. I stopped in for my second *sello*, or stamp for my *credencial*. With my mission accomplished, I turned left from the albergue's gate and saw a yellow arrow on a wall directly in front of me.

The arrow sent me up the highway a bit and then down some back streets. Cars sat in front of the houses, most of which were dark. Occasionally a security light would turn on and show the way. Feeling like an interloper, I experienced an anxious awareness as I strolled through the sleeping neighborhood. Then I heard the tapping of walking poles on the pavement and the hushed conversation of a Japanese couple passing me. The streets started to descend. The houses became further apart, and the trail opened to a stairway that led to a path at the beach.

I came upon the Japanese couple standing at the top. Their cameras were in hand to capture the unusual pre-dawn vista. The sun hadn't risen yet, and the silver moon, two days past full, hung over the water to the west. It cast a shimmering trail of light across the water beckoning all who saw it to whatever lay beyond the horizon. I could see the waves crashing against a rocky coastline with their spray reaching into the lightening sky. I marveled in silence at my good luck to be able to capture this moment.

Just a week and a half before I stood somewhere beyond the moon on the shore of Long Beach Island in New Jersey scanning the horizon on a cloudless afternoon. I got a weird feeling and pointed with my finger and told my girlfriend at my side, "That's where I'm going. That's where I'll be in a few days, walking along this ocean and looking back to where we are now." As I descended the stairs, I thought about that moment.

I continued to walk down the stairs, stopping several times to look at the sea again and not wanting the view to end. As I reached the bottom, the Japanese couple still clicked pictures above. The Camino route took me past Playa Grande, probably one of the few sandy spots in the area. A concrete breakwater protected the closed bathhouse and other buildings that faced the sea. The Camino then followed the access road for the beach. Campers lined the road along the way with no one stirring inside any of them. What a shame that, being where they were, they slept through the glorious show the moon directed at their doorsteps.

The sun slowly crept into the sky behind the shadowed hills on the eastern side of the highway above. Finally, the Camino left the access road and started to follow a dirt path along the water. It wound its way through fields bounded by stone walls, and I could hear the constant sound of crashing surf to the left.

Golden fields, full with dried grass fronted the path, but there were no animals grazing. Occasionally a farm road or path would lead up an incline toward a house, the highway, or down toward the coast. At times, there were abandoned structures. After about 3 kilometers, a fort, long ago destroyed by the sea, formed a tiny promontory sticking out into the waves. Just beyond an abandoned farm, the Camino diverged from the path along the coast and headed up a steep paved driveway toward the highway. At the top it followed a wooded dirt road parallel to the highway passing small farms whose fields tumbled down to the coastline.

At 4.2 kilometers, the foot path joined the highway bike path for a while. As I strolled along, other pilgrims, later risers, started to pass me, including the Japanese couple. You see, I've always been a slow walker. One of the reasons I walked alone was that I knew I would frustrate anyone walking with me. However, I can be very competitive, and the thought of people passing me irked me all through the Camino. The sound of footsteps behind me caused me to pick up the pace, but to no avail. They always left me in the dust.

For anyone who has been to the west coast of Ireland, this area would look familiar. It reminded me of the Dingle Peninsula, without its winding, narrow roads, but with its rocky, wild coast and small farms surrounded by stone walls. The Celts who settled here long ago and transformed the culture and language must have felt right at home.

The mountain, Sta Tecla, which rises south of A Guarda, is the site of an ancient Celtic community called a *castro*. However, some of the most obvious pieces of evidence of Celtic presence are the symbols carved in stone and elsewhere, as well as the common small raised buildings used for grain storage called *horreos*, which I also saw in Ireland. The Gallician language has Gaelic and Portuguese Roots, and while almost no one speaks Gaelic, there are still Gaelic words in use.

While walking along the highway, I conversed for a few moments with an American woman who appeared to be in her forties, and then a Spanish man out for his morning exercise. For the first time I could feel the heat of the sun that peeked over the hills. I felt fresh. The excitement of being on the Camino, along with the beautiful weather spurred me on. I knew I'd soon be at my first rest stop and the thought of a second cup of coffee also motivated me.

The stretch between A Guarda and the village of Oia is about 12.5 kilometers. Oia is a few kilometers south of my destination, Viladesuso. There are very few services along the route. The first one is at the midway point to Oia, a dot on the map called Portecelo. There's a religious monument there, but the café that showed on Google Maps interested me more.

The Camino to Portecelo left the highway via a dirt road. I passed a few local people out walking and working along the road, as the little place began to stir. Just before the dirt road ended, a cluster of Pilgrims sat at plastic tables at a roadside stand. The place sat perched above the few houses that dotted a road leading down to the ocean. I recognized almost everyone at the cafe because they had already passed me. There were knowing nods of recognition, as I walked amongst them to take my place in the queue to get coffee.

This rest stop was little more than a shack with a few tables. Several women manned the coffee machine and greeted customers. There were packaged snacks and a menu that listed sandwiches.

While waiting for my coffee, I struck up a brief conversation with a man from New England. But with coffee in-hand, I took a seat alone looking over the sea down the hill. The plastic seat helped relieve my tiring feet, and I stretched my legs in front of me, and marveled at how well I felt. I had walked about 6.7 kilometers. In reality, 6.7 kilometers had been a light training day, and I felt confident about the next 10 kilometers to Viladesuso.

Every once in a while, all the way to Santiago, I would find myself overwhelmed by the places I found myself and the reality of my walking the Camino. As my eyes swept over the view of the ocean and the other pilgrims, the months of solo training back in Mexico seemed far away and long ago. The distance I had chosen to walk seemed unfathomable. I had no idea what might befall me in the days ahead, but I felt excited that my pilgrimage had finally started.

I reached into my day pack and pulled out the snack the hotel had prepared for me. It contained a ham and cheese sandwich, a package of cookies and a banana. I ate the simple sandwich and banana, savoring each bite, and washing them down with water. I decided to save the cookies for later.

The Japanese couple sat on a bench tying the sneakers they had taken off. We talked briefly. It so happened that they didn't plan to walk the Camino at all. They had been on vacation in Spain and with a few days left and an adventurous spirit, decided to walk the Camino route for something different to do. They didn't know how far they would go – only that they needed to be back in Madrid on a certain date.

10 A PERFECT DAY TO START
A CAMINO

My stay at the rest stop seemed longer than a scant 15 minutes, but I knew I should start walking again before I stiffened up too much. Slowly lifting myself from the chair, I felt a little stiff, as I usually did after a rest. I grabbed my pack and ambled up the hill to meet the continuation of the path near the highway.

At this stage of my walk, I still felt an overwhelming excitement and happiness about where I found myself, and felt no need for personal interaction with others. As I walked, I constantly mused about the beauty of the ocean and the hills, or went over the logistics of getting to Viladesuso, or through the next day, and the next week.

Later in my pilgrimage, I concluded that most of the conversations I had with other pilgrims seemed pretty mundane, shallow and inconsequential. Usually the topics would include: where people came from; where they started their Camino; how long had they been walking; to what destination they were heading for that day. Rarely did it get even as deep as *why* are you walking. Maybe I just didn't care or they weren't forthcoming.

It seemed to me conversations seemed to be like strange dogs meeting and smelling each other's rear ends to get acquainted. Once the connection is established they go their separate ways leaving each other alone. While I welcomed occasional social interaction for a change, for the most part, I walked in quiet contemplation. In my case, I wouldn't characterize it as "spiritual" until much later in the pilgrimage. It appeared to me that pilgrims, especially those walking alone, were involved in their own thoughts, emotions, or dealing with physical pain. Most that I met didn't seem very interested in talking at length. Even at cafes, people didn't care to talk much, being more interested in caring for their own bodies and thoughts than talking about them.

***

From Portecelo to Oia the Camino pretty much follows the highway. The sun had now passed over the hills to the east, and it surprised me how hot it had already gotten at this early hour on a late September day. The summer of 2018 had been unusually hot in Europe, and summer's departure demonstrated a grudging obstinacy. The beads of sweat formed on my face and arms. I pulled my Tilly hat down so it covered the back of my neck.

It seemed like the perfect day to start a Camino. I had heard stories of people having to deal with rain, cold, and even snow on their first day. But, here in Galicia, you couldn't find a cloud in the sky. The temperature had risen to the mid-70s F, and you could feel a constant breeze.

Just before Oia, the Camino headed down a lane lined with 8 foot high rock walls adorned with flowers. Colors of brilliant orange, yellow, and fuchsia awakened the eyes, and fragrant smells intoxicated the breeze from the nearby Atlantic. Oia is on a little bay, and the path followed the curve of the hill that surrounds it. Around a bend, I saw the large Monastery, built in 1137, that dominates the picturesque little town. The Monastery sat like a postcard photo in the brilliant noonday sun, framed in the blue of a cloudless sky.

The flowery lane ran into the village, and became a narrow winding street lined with two story homes. They turned the way into a cool and shadowed path. I planned to find the village plaza and rest before getting my *credencial* stamped at the monastery. However, a small café/bar, Casa Henriqueta, appeared around a corner where several Spanish men sipped beers and several pilgrims rested their weary bones. There were no outside tables left so I ventured inside the dark cavernous bar area where I sat and propped myself against the stone wall of the building.

The sweat rolled down my forehead and turned my armpits wet. The cool temperature in the shade of the bar, made me feel chilly. The cold beers that the locals drank looked enticing, but I stuck with coffee and ate the cookies from my snack. The pilgrims in the place appeared to be a multi-national group, and spoke in several languages. I tried to figure out where they were from. Once again, no one said much, everyone concentrating on their own thoughts. I hadn't talked with anyone for several kilometers, but even though a conversation would be interesting, I didn't have the energy to make an effort.

My destination in Viladesuso lay only 3.7 kilometers away – *a hop, skip, and a jump* – I tried to convince myself. I had walked 12.6 kilometers, the upper reaches of my training walks. A weary, resigned tiredness accompanied me as I paid my bill and the cashier stamped my *credencial*. Somewhat rested and stamped, I felt no need to find the plaza or visit the monastery. My thoughts were set on reaching my destination.

The Camino followed the breakwater at the foot of the monastery and started up a hill to the right passing a scattering of houses. The path continued down a dirt road past more farms and through wooded areas. It seemed that almost every farm had a vegetable garden where there were rows of tall stalks, stripped of their leaves. At first I thought they were brussel sprouts. Strangely though, if this were the land of brussel sprouts, they never appeared on any menus and I did not find them mentioned in my research. I later found out that the stalks were collards. Collards are used to make Sopa Gallega, a regional specialty soup made with collards and white beans that is often found on menus del dia.

As I walked, I began passing groups of women, leaning against walls, and huddling in their shade, doing some kind of handiwork. They wore rubber working gloves, handling the contents of buckets of black shells, and chattered among themselves. After passing several groups, I stopped to ask what they were doing, and they informed me that they were cleaning barnacles and readying them for market. The ocean and its crashing waves were only a couple hundred meters away. It must have been past low tide when the women would have climbed out on the rocks to gather their harvest.

Gooseneck Barnacles, or *percebes* as the Spaniards call them, are a prized delicacy in Galicia. There are probably as many ways to prepare them as there are cooks, but the primary way is to boil them in seawater just long enough to loosen them from their shells. Then, you remove them from their shells with your fingers or suck them from the shell directly into your mouth. You can also add them to other preparations. When cooked properly, they have a salty sweetness.

The dirt road ended at the highway. I had been there before on Google Street View. My destination, *Alojamiento Camino Portugues*, a private *albergue,* beckoned only a half kilometer north. I desperately wanted relief from the brutal sun, and rest couldn't come soon enough. Taking a large gulp of water, I pressed on. Viladesuso, at this point is basically a highway with a few hotels and restaurants facing the sea. I felt envious of the people in the hotel pools and restaurants I passed. The Hotel Glascow, across the street from the *albergue* dominated the view with its multiple floors and big ugly sign. As I got closer to the sign, I could see the *Alojamiento* on the other side of the road, and crossed the highway.

Entering the door, the place looked deserted, but the cool temperature welcomed me. I was either the first one there or all the visitors were elsewhere having lunch or napping in the dormitory. This *albergue* had a dormitory and several private rooms one of which I had reserved. I'd be sharing two bathrooms with other private room guests. After ringing a bell at the desk, a young man came down the stairs, checked me in, and led me to my room on the second floor. I returned with him downstairs to retrieve my backpack which, to my relief, Tuitrans had delivered safely.

My private room looked just like it appeared on the *albergue's* website, simple with a double bed, and comfortable mattress. It faced the highway and commanded a view of the Atlantic Ocean across the street.

I had survived the first day's walk. Now I needed a substantial meal. After cleaning up, the clerk suggested the menu del dia at the Hotel Costa Verde, a short walk up the highway. Still dressed for walking, the hotel looked a bit intimidating, and I thought I might be a little under-dressed.

I found myself walking there with a short-haired woman whom I engaged in conversation. She appeared to be in her fifties, wearing tan shorts and a striped golf shirt. She happened to be staying at the Costa Verde, and planned to meet some people there for lunch and a reunion of sorts. When we reached the front door, she joined her party on the patio. Four of the people including the woman had been walking the Camino from Porto. Two old friends living in Spain drove to Viladesuso to meet them. The woman introduced me to the group, but I quickly forgot their names. The group moved inside to a large round table. I decided to stay on the patio for lunch rather than eat inside. Under the awning where I sat, the ocean breezes cooled the air, and I preferred to observe the few happenings along the highway.

As often occurs on the Camino, these chance meetings turn into short-lived friendships that last a few days or the rest of the pilgrimage. I'll call this group of pilgrims the "Four Amigos." And for the next ten days our paths crossed many times all the way to and in Santiago.

For lunch, I decided on the menu del dia, and was surprised when the waiter arrived with a half-liter of chilled white wine. I sipped it as I, waited for another substantial lunch. It started with *sopa gallega*, more *merluza*, and finished with a cool refreshing flan. When I lived in the states, I rarely ordered white fish from the Atlantic like hake or cod. I never bought them in the grocery store either. They always tasted fishy. On the rare occasion when I ate them, a friend would have just caught them, and cooked them for the next meal. One thing about eating fish in Galicia is that it tastes so fresh, and most cooks prepare it perfectly. The big meal with the wine wooed me back to my room for a shower and nap.

11 WALKING ON THE HIGHWAY

The alarm on my cell phone went off at 6:00 am. I lay in the darkness wiggling my toes and stretching. Swinging my feet over the side of the bed, I began to assess my condition, and found my feet and legs in good shape. I walked to the window in search of the moon and the ocean. I saw no repeat of yesterday's pre-dawn show. A cloud of fog blanketed the still sleeping village. The only lights were the sign at the Glascow Hotel and occasional car headlights piercing the fog.

From my months of training, I had developed a routine to prepare me for the day's walk. I first taped my heels to prevent blisters. Then I slipped on ankle supports, socks, and finally trail-walking sneakers. Throughout the Camino the only adjustments I needed to make were on occasional days when I would tape my ankles or arches. For the most part, I never had serious problems with my feet and never a blister.

When I left the room, darkness enveloped the albergue.

51

I fished on the wall with my hand to find the light for the stairs, and descended to the front desk. After placing my backpack behind it, I stepped out into the damp, dark morning and started walking north. Just beyond the Costa Verde, the lights illuminated a bar/café where I had had a drink and snack for dinner the night before. I entered for my customary coffee and croissant. At this early hour, a collection of locals read their newspapers and sipped coffee.

This day, Thursday, September 27, I'd be following Highway 552 up the coast all the way to the town of Baiona, a touristy town with a fishing history and several historical sites. According to the maps, it would be about a 14 kilometer walk. There were two ways I could go. The official Camino leaves the highway 5 kilometers beyond Viladesuso, just after a town called Mougas. The trail goes up a rocky path for 2 kilometers, along the crest of the mountain, and then down to Baiona. The alternative route follows the bike path along the ocean. I had read descriptions and seen videos of the official route and decided, because of my hip, not to risk injury on the official route. Regardless, the distance was the same.

Walking on the highway wasn't how I originally thought about walking the Camino. I thought that it would follow ancient paths through bucolic woodland and rural panoramas. While there are many places where you can experience that idyllic vision, the route makes accommodations for the encroachment of modern civilization. This was especially true on my walk this day. It would mostly be on the highway.

So, I started walking down the highway north out of Viladesuso. It jogged to the left and then the right following the coastline before ascending a long hill. The muted light from the fog and ocean mist gave the morning an eerie feeling. The highway then descended for a kilometer along a marshy stretch. Everything looked gray. North of the marsh, the Camino turned left and wound its way through a group of homes where no one stirred, and past an *albergue* which still looked dark inside. When the path met the highway again the elevation started to rise, and the fog began to lift. The still gray sky seemed to hover low over the road while I walked uphill past numerous motels and RV resorts that sat on a cliff overlooking the Atlantic somewhere behind the mist below.

At the crest of the hill I came upon a small shop selling pilgrimage souvenirs and paraphernalia. I had been wondering where the pilgrims I saw got their scallop shells with the cross of Saint James.

Scallop shells can be found along the coast of Galicia, and there are many legends about how and why the scallop shell became a significant symbol for pilgrims dating back to the time when they took the body of Saint James from Jerusalem to Spain. Pilgrims in medieval times wore the scallop shell as a symbol of the pilgrimage, and it could double as a scoop or bowl during meals.

Today the shell is a souvenir worn by pilgrims as a badge of pilgrimage, and often accompanies or replaces the yellow arrow in the signage marking the Camino route.

I hadn't been looking for a shell. But, then I found this

shop. You could have mistaken the proprietor for one of the original pilgrims. He looked like an older man with a slight, but muscular build, and a well-chiseled face. I asked him about the shop, and he told me that his mission was to help pilgrims, and that he used all the money he raised for charity. I bought one of his shells, and he handed me a free map. After thanking him and throwing a few Euros in a donation jar, I tied the shell to my daypack and resumed my walk.

The bike path descended a ways along cliffs overlooking the now visible ocean. The road ahead bent to the left and several buildings appeared to be hanging on to the cliff. The hills rose steeply on the east side of the road. Even though they would appear green in the sunlight, the shadows from the hill painted them a dull flat gray.

I began to hear the tap, tap, tap of walking poles striking the pavement behind me. The rhythm told me that the walkers were moving at a fast clip. Turning my head I saw two women dressed in gray as dull as the morning. They approached carrying on a spirited conversation. We exchanged a few words commenting on the weather. Then they forged ahead leaving me to my solitude.

Around the bend and up another rise a small roadside hotel clung to the cliff. As I approached the Hotel Soremmo, several pilgrims sat at umbrella covered tables having coffee, including the two women in gray. I got myself a coffee and asked them if I could join them. They were a mother who looked to be in her late fifties and her thirty-something daughter. The mother had travelled from South Africa to join her England-based daughter to walk the Camino. While the mother had walked the French Camino before, the daughter had never walked one. They had been walking for 21 days since leaving Lisbon, and they wanted to fulfill their goal for the day by completing another 30 kilometers.

The women went on their way, leaving me there to finish my coffee. Just beyond the hotel, the Camino took a sharp left turn, almost reversing itself, down a steep hill behind the hotel. It ended at the ocean where three men, dressed in sweat shirts, fished while smoking cigarettes. A marshy trail continued north through rocks. Several pilgrims had stopped to look for shells. After a short while, the trail ended at a gravel road that bordered Camping Mougas and Albergue Solidario, and went up a hill to the highway.

I remembered this junction from Google Street View too. This juncture presented a major decision point for me. Straight ahead, a yellow arrow directed pilgrims up a driveway and into a field where the official Camino route continued steeply into the woods.

12 THE LOST STRANGER

Because of my hip and what I had read about the condition of the official trail for the next few kilometers, I had decided to take an alternative route. So, I ignored the yellow arrow pointing up the hill, and turned left to continue north along Highway 552. The supposed high point of the official route was a fantastic view of the surrounding country, the lighthouse on Monte de Bareda, and the picturesque Cies Islands at the mouth of the Vigo River. As I soon found out, I may have missed the bird's eye view, but I walked around the mountain and lighthouse, and could see the islands from the road.

By now, the sun appeared over the mountains to the east in full force. A cloudless bright blue sky reflected on the ocean below the highway. The road followed a cliff and, for the most part, gave me an unobstructed view of the Atlantic's wide expanse. As I passed a group of cliff-hanging houses, dogs barked from the other sides of gates, and a man washed his car in a driveway. Monte de Bareda rose a few kilometers ahead while a sprawling hotel complex, Talasco Atlantico, hugged its base where the road bent to the left to circumvent the mountain.

Except for some cyclists passing me, I thought I might be the only pilgrim walking this route. Then I heard more tapping behind me. A young blonde-haired woman in shorts and a tank top started to catch up to me. I wondered why a person who looked fit enough to climb the hill I had avoided, would be taking the "easy" route. She pulled alongside me, and asked in English, "Does this route go to Baiona?"

It must have been obvious that I was North American, otherwise why ask me in English? I soon found out she was from Germany.

"Yes," I told her. "This is the Camino bike route, and it goes around that mountain up there and follows the coast to Baiona." I pointed to Mount Bareda looming ahead, and wondered why she had set out on this route without knowing if it would get her to where she wanted to go.

"Why are you walking on the bicycle route?" She asked. I told her about my reasons for choosing it, and then asked her the same question.

"Oh, it's a long story. You probably wouldn't be interested," she replied before launching into her tale.

For the next 2 kilometers we walked together. I think she needed to talk with someone, and I happened to be the only one around. She walked faster than me, forcing me to pick up my pace. I didn't mind. By now, I welcomed a conversation that took me out of my own thoughts, and I found it easier to walk faster with someone to talk with.

As we talked, her choice of route became evident.

A lot of people walk the Camino to escape a bad situation. The woman had taken a leave from her job in a bookstore after breaking up with a long-time boyfriend. She had started the Camino in Lisbon and had been walking for a couple of weeks. Along the way, she had met someone special. On any other day they would have walked together. Today she needed some distance, so she got up early and left the albergue before him. Knowing that he would follow the Camino up the hill and over the mountain in pursuit, she took the highway route.

She had talked with the new boyfriend about extending their relationship when they returned home, but felt hesitant because it seemed too soon after her break-up, and they lived an hour away from each other. What would happen if she returned home and the old boyfriend wanted to get together again? What if she got home and the relationship with the new boyfriend didn't work out?

I listened, and counseled that we never know for certain how relationships will play themselves out, but you never find out unless you try. I suggested that, if she really liked the new guy, she should take the relationship wherever it goes.

We walked together around the base of Monte de Bareda. On the other side, we stopped alongside a roundabout in the shade of a road embankment. A road went up the mountain to the lighthouse where a trail connected to the main Camino route. To the left, a path led to a viewing area over the ocean. The Cies Islands stood majestically out to sea in the distance. Straight ahead, Highway 552 continued to Baiona, my destination. As I sipped some water, she busied herself on her cell phone, probably arranging a rendezvous with her new friend. We parted and I never saw her again.

The highway snaked along the side of the mountain that rose from the sea with numerous scenic turn-offs and picnic areas. Bend after wide sweeping bend, it continued until it straightened into a residential area. *One more bend, maybe two and I'd be in Baiona,* I thought. The signs told a different story: 3 kilometers, 2 kilometers, 1 kilometer. Finally, as tourist restaurants and hotels appeared on the hillside, I knew the town had to be getting close. Then around a final bend, the Monument to Diego Carmono and Vasco Gallego appeared ahead. They were two local sailors that sailed with Magellan on his circumnavigation of the globe. The now parking meter-lined street straightened into an urban scene with hotels, apartment buildings, restaurants, and stores on the right side, and a park on the water side to the left.

13 REST DAY IN BAIONA

My hotel, Hotel Cais, was a few blocks ahead, just before a roundabout. As I walked, tables with umbrellas lined the street and the cafes were getting full. I nodded to a couple sitting under an umbrella whom I had seen having coffee at the Hotel Soremmo. Recognizing me, they nodded back.

The door to the hotel on the main street opened into a bar, where a noon-time group of men traded stories and watched *futbol* games on TV while sipping bottles of beer. The bartender saw me with my daypack and walking poles and pointed me through doors that entered into the lobby of the hotel. My backpack awaited me. After check-in, I took the stairs to my room on the second floor. I found a bright room with a double bed, writing desk, and private bath. A window opened on a narrow walking street lined with restaurants, shops and bars, *Rua Ventura Misa*.

Initially, I had doubts about how my body would do after two back-to-back days of walking. At 16.7 and 14 kilometers, they would be the shortest distances of the entire walk. I had decided to spend two nights at Hotel Cais and rest my legs and feet before three 20 kilometer walking days to Pontevedra. Besides, I knew I would have to do a load of laundry. I had built in another rest day for Pontevedra before pushing on to Santiago.

Baiona has a rich history and occupies a strategic position at the head of the Vigo River. Over the centuries dating back before the birth of Christ, a succession of armies conquered the location, including Julius Caesar in 60 BC. Mont Real, a fortress built in the 15th century, lords over the harbor and today serves as a Parador, a high-end hotel, run by the Spanish government.

Modern Baiona is a touristy beach town with small hotels and restaurants lining the main street and an historic quarter which runs inland behind it. While there is still a fishing industry, a recreational marina is most prominent along the harbor.

I needed to get some lunch, so I perused the restaurants and menus along Ventura Misa and entered a busy restaurant, *Recuncho Marineiro,* decorated with nautical décor, a long wooden counter and white wooden tables. The walls were plastered with chalk boards displaying a dazzling selection of seafood choices and other Galician specialties and wines. I sat at a side-counter and ordered the 12 Euro menu del dia. Lunch started with a salmon paté, and then a gigantic portion of marinated cubed roasted pork with roasted potatoes, wine, dessert, and coffee. I returned that evening, opting for an outside high-top table where I ate fried calamari.

The next morning, I went in search of a laundromat and back-tracked along the main street several blocks. There I turned left up a side street making note of several cafes to have breakfast. After stuffing my clothes in a washing machine, I took a seat at a café/bakery with decadent looking pastries, and used the time to write my first email journal.

Before I left for Europe I explored several ways to communicate with family and friends in the U.S. and Mexico. My tech skills are basic. My tablet didn't have a keyboard and I couldn't find a Bluetooth one that would work. For that reason, I thought blogging would take too much time and effort. So, I decided to write a brief email recap of my adventures, and the day off in Baiona allowed me enough time to bring everyone up-to-date.

When the laundry was finished, I took a little detour, to find a bus station that I heard was around the corner. I decided to inquire about the early morning schedule the next day. I needed to take a bus towards Vigo, but I would be getting off in a town called A Ramallasa only 4-5 kilometers down the road. The clerk told me that the first bus left at 7 am. That would be perfect.

14 WALKING TO MY ABILITIES

The hotel lobby was empty when I started my third walking day, Saturday, September 29. The bar/café in the front room hadn't opened yet either. I slipped out a door that opened on a walkway to the main street and bus stop. I had a few minutes before the bus would arrive at seven. I shuddered in the morning cold waiting in the dark. A woman already waited at the bus stop. She looked as if she were carrying a bag of cleaning supplies. I presumed she was going to work.

My walk today promised to be challenging, for several reasons. First was the walking distance from Baiona to Vigo of more than 30 kilometers – way beyond my limit. Second, according to my confusing map, the Camino split into numerous branches as it passed through the sprawling suburbs south of Vigo. The official route winds its way inland. But my map showed at least three optional routes - one a handicap route and another route for bicycles. They hugged the shoreline with its gentler elevations and stayed on paved streets. In some parts, they followed the same streets. Whichever way I chose, the distance would be challenging, and I wondered whether I'd be able to complete what could be a very long day.

To make the day more manageable, I decided to skip the first 5 kilometers of the day's route from Baiona to A Ramallosa by taking a bus. At the end of my day's walk, I would be either at the futbol stadium or at Parque de Castrelos, a major city park. I planned to take another bus from there to my hotel in Vigo, downtown near the harbor. The next day I would return by taxi to pick up the trail again. From what I had read, it was a difficult, long, and hilly walk to the port area from where the Camino passes through the city. It would have added several painful kilometers onto the day.

When the almost empty bus to Vigo arrived, I stepped up and asked the driver to leave me off at the bridge in A Ramallosa. In less than ten minutes, the bus left me standing near a roundabout at the east end of Ponte de Ramallosa. The street lights at the roundabout lit the still dark morning a fluorescent, eye squinting brightness. As usual at this time of day, I started searching for my first cup of coffee. I found a yellow arrow which pointed the way uphill to an albergue and the official Camino route. But, I'd be following the bicycle route closer to the shore. A Ramallosa appeared dead at this hour. I couldn't find any place to get coffee. So I started walking down a broad street, lined first by a park near the mouth of the Rio Miñor, then by apartment building after apartment building. I figured that there had to be a café somewhere ahead.

Walking in the dark on a deserted major street before 8:00 am felt strange. An occasional car or bus would pass by. I expected the police to stop me to ask me what I was doing in this neighborhood at this hour. Probably, they were used to seeing people with day packs, shorts, and walking poles on this route, but it didn't reduce my anxiety. I would have felt more comfortable in daylight.

Just before eight, I came to an intersection that showed signs of life. Playa Americana, with a small commercial area of shops, restaurants, and two story apartment buildings lay a few steps off the route bordering the sea. Customers waited for the corner café, Xuntos, to open at 8. By now I needed a bite to eat and began to suffer from caffeine deprivation. So, I joined the locals in anticipation of breakfast and a warm place to sit.

After getting back on the road, the apartment buildings faded and I started passing middle class, two-story homes with white walls and orange tiled roofs. Kilometer after kilometer and roundabout after roundabout I continued walking. At each roundabout I consulted my map. I knew, at some point, I had to turn left to get to the beach. However, after such a long time, I became worried that I'd missed the cut-off. Now mind you, it didn't matter if I walked the route along the beach. If I just stayed on the same street, the route from the beach would re-join it in a few kilometers. To be frank, walking on the highway started to get boring, and I looked forward to seeing the ocean again.

When I got to the village of Nigran, I consulted my map. Nigran's center, sort of an antiseptic city planners dream, contained several blocks of two story new red brick buildings like many gentrified small-town centers in the states. The map told me I should turn left to the beach about a kilometer ahead.

As I walked, there were no signs pointing the way, and since this route didn't follow the official Camino, no yellow arrows either. Looking for the right street became problematic. As I passed each street I would wonder whether I should take this street or the next one. I decided on a winding street heading downhill that looked as good as any of the others. Pristine suburban homes lined it. I didn't see a soul as I walked down the empty street. I'm not accustomed to walking in strange neighborhoods, even in broad daylight. I wondered if the people behind the curtains were curious about the tap, tap, tap of my walking poles and the strange person carrying them. At the bottom of the hill, the street ended near the community center at the west end of Panxon Beach.

It must have been 9:30, but there were very few people out walking, even on the *malecon* (boardwalk). Maybe the day's grayness and damp mist, which hid the view of the ocean, kept them indoors. With the damp, cool, breeze coming off the water, I could understand how fair-weather walkers and joggers might opt for another cup of coffee while waiting for the sun to burn off the fog and warm things up a bit.

I followed the malecon to the end at the village of Panxon. A paved road continued over a hill, through a commercial area until it reached Playa Pato, another stretch of beach without a malecon and less commercial.

The route left the pavement and proceeded down a dirt road. A middle-aged couple bundled for the damp weather, warned me not to take a path down to the beach. Rather I should stay on the dirt road and turn up the hill at the next chance.

I began to realize that I had very few navigational aids to help me find out where I was going. My map didn't show a lot of detail, and I couldn't get the GPS on my phone to work. GPS would have come in very handy while walking this section. While it appeared on the map as a bicycle route, it had no yellow arrows to point the way. I felt a little uneasy to be walking in a strange place without a clue. Every intersection became a major decision point, and would remain so until I rejoined the main Camino route.

The steep hill that climbed from the beach back to the highway made the muscles in my legs burn with each step. The narrow road split, leaving me with a decision about which fork to follow. I went left in the direction I had been traveling. After a short walk, I found myself back on the main road I had left earlier. After a few more kilometers, I stopped at a panaderia just off the main street around 10:00. The sugar and cinnamon smells of fresh-baked goodies that wafted out of the kitchen made my mouth water and promised a welcome break. I ordered more coffee and a fresh-baked croissant.

A few minutes after resuming my walk, I changed my plans on-the-fly and made a fateful decision, which would affect the rest of my Camino experience. Walking in the bike path had been satisfactory. Physically I felt fine. The bike path would take me on suburban and city streets to the Rio Legares, and then follow the river to the stadium. At the river, I would also have an option to follow another alternative route along the harbor that would take me downtown.

15 FATEFUL CHANGE OF PLANS

After leaving the panaderia, I noticed a street on my right that angled off the main road and climbed a hill. Four pilgrims started to climb it.

I wondered why they headed in that direction, so I consulted my map, and discovered that the route they were taking converged with the official Camino after a few kilometers. I pondered whether I should chance it. I had this weird, guilty feeling about not walking the official route, and also I thought I could use a change of scenery. The way up the hill promised a new adventure, hopefully away from the trucks and cars and sprawling suburbia. So, I followed the four pilgrims up the hill.

I quickly lost the four in front of me who walked at a much faster pace. Occasional groups of farmhouses now bordered the rural way. The route twisted and turned and there were numerous junctions that had me puzzled. Occasionally, I got lucky because, on this route, there were some markers pointing toward the official route.

Eventually, I reached Highway N-552 where I happily saw a yellow arrow on a wall pointing the way downhill and to the left.

According to my map, I needed to find a factory called Naves Industries. After a few hundred meters, a turn-off led to a nameless industrial type building perched on a hill at the end of a driveway. Supposedly, the official Camino route passed behind it. According to Google Maps, the factory happened to be a few hundred meters shy of the "100 kilometer to Santiago" marker. That is the minimum distance required to complete the Camino to earn a compostela.

I couldn't see anyone on the factory's property and the building appeared closed. There were no cars or trucks visible. A chain link fence with an open gate stood to the right of the building. I stood at the bottom of the driveway questioning whether I should go up. I wondered if I would be trespassing. In reality, I had no other choice. So, I hiked up the driveway to the back of the building where I saw plastic and steel drums stacked all over. I stopped and looked for a yellow arrow. It took me a little while, but I found it.

A narrow overgrown path, that didn't look much like a Camino route, led into the woods. Even though thousands had traversed this path before, I felt as though I were bushwhacking as I dove into the unknown. The path ran on a hill above N-552, and the noise from the traffic broke the peacefulness of the route. The shade of the tall trees that bordered the path through the woods made walking more comfortable. As I walked, the way became wider. It joined other hiking trails that crossed from the hill above. Walking on the dirt and stones seemed like a new sensation to my feet. I needed to take much more care about where I walked. The path went up hills and down. For the first time, I needed my walking poles for help on the hills and to keep my balance. I took my time, thinking that it would take me at least twice as long to walk the same distance in the woods as on the bike path. I began to regret diverting from the bicycle route.

On descending one of those hills, I ran across a washed out section of the trail with numerous large rocks, along with steep and deep natural stairs formed by tree roots. I needed to be very careful navigating my way down. As I picked my way through, suddenly, one of my walking poles slipped and I lurched to the left - twisting my body, but breaking a fall.

Recovering my balance, I stopped and winced in pain. The suddenness of the mishap shook me. My thoughts were scrambled and, feeling out of control, as adrenalin pumped through my body, a sense of panic swept over me.

It took a minute to gather myself as I stood, leaning on my poles, in the middle of "who knows where" and alone.

I remember thinking that this was a close call. If I had fallen, it could have been a lot worse. I could have twisted or dislocated my recently replaced right hip. I could have broken the hip or another limb. I felt lucky, but not too lucky. When I gathered my wits and started to walk again, the muscles on the left side of my back hurt at every step.

At the time, I couldn't have known that, whatever I had

done to myself that morning, would affect the rest of my Camino, and I still had seven walking days to go to get to Santiago.

When the path broke out of the woods into what seemed like a suburban subdivision, I sat down on a rock wall to rest and adjust my equipment. I felt pain at every move. At this point, I couldn't stop. I had to move on. So, I reached in my daypack, found an ibuprofen, and downed it with water.

The pavement continued downhill until it joined the highway where I turned right. A half kilometer further, I reached an intersection where a substantial café stood on the shady side of the street, Panaderia Pasteleria D'Casal. I had walked about 14 kilometers, but it seemed a lot longer. Besides needing a good rest, I was hungry. So, at the panaderia, the sight of empanadas in the display case made me happy. I ordered one and sat with a fresh, ice-cold bottle of water, loosened my sneakers, stretched my legs, and savored every morsel. Afterwards, I sat for what seemed like an unusually long time watching people and the traffic.

When I started my training, a few months earlier in the summer, I liked to begin my walks early, often before the sun came up. That way I could avoid most of the heat that got intense after noon. I often would stop for breakfast along the way, but quickly found that the more I ate the more difficult it became to comfortably finish the walk. One of my favorite stops during training became a French patisserie four kilometers from my house. Their croissants, made with butter, left my fingers greasy, but tended to last me for at least 2-3 hours of walking. So I got in the habit of just snacking. On the Camino, breakfast consisted of a croissant and coffee. Most days I bought an empanada to eat around noon. Empanadas are found everywhere in the Spanish-speaking world. They are usually a baked turnover that can have a meat or fruit filling.

Somewhat refreshed after my snack, I started walking again down N-552 towards Vigo. It was a busy, noisy, and commercial hodge-podge, lined by hardware and furniture stores, supermarkets, auto dealerships and other buildings. N-552 could take me all the way to the stadium in Vigo, but the Camino diverted to the right near a major intersection at Highway VG-20. Somehow, I missed the yellow arrow, but I didn't care. I wanted to get to the stadium and public transportation the fastest and most direct way possible. Being out of the woods and the start of the afternoon, I began to feel hot now, especially from the heat reflecting pavement. My back added to the discomfort of walking.

I found this stretch of commercial sprawl the most unpleasant of my Camino. At one point I'm sure it was a pretty rural road like many others on the way to Santiago. I couldn't find any redeeming qualities about it, and I'm sure it challenges many preconceived notions of an idyllic pilgrimage past fields, vineyards, and charming little towns. There is no way that pilgrims of decades and centuries ago could foresee the changes that the route would undergo or even plan for them. Modern pilgrims have no choice but to tolerate what history has left them.

Step after step in the hot sun, I just kept walking down

N-552. *When is this going to end*, I kept thinking, as I tried to keep my attention focused on anything but my sore back. My feet felt fine, but my legs were weary. At about 17 kilometers, the bike path crossed N-552. Later I looked at the map and retraced my walk. When I compared the distance I had walked to that of the bike path, it was almost the same. I can't help thinking that my original plan to walk the bike path would have been a lot easier.

The bike path continued along the east side of the Rio Legares, which at this point looked like more of a stream than a river. The sidewalk continued on the west side. I sat on a bench in the shade to rest, and surveyed my location. A sprawling complex of buildings surrounded by a high white wall occupied the other side of the highway. Later I found out it was a Peugot/Citroen car factory. Heavy traffic on the highway filled the air with choking exhaust. Picking myself up, I continued until I soon looked up to see the 29,000 seat Estadio Balaidios, home of Real Club Celta futbol team. In my research, I knew that I could find a bus there to take me to the port area. The stadium was big, and I didn't know where to find a bus stop. Making matters worse, I did not have a bus schedule.

So I walked the length of the stadium to a multi-cornered intersection trying to figure out where to go next. I saw yellow arrows for the Camino and followed them across the street. At this point, I made a big mistake. I should have asked someone where to find a bus or taxi because, from my vantage point, I didn't see a likely place. Thousands of people came here by public transportation, but I couldn't find the bus stop!

16 FRUSTRATION IN VIGO

It was close to three o'clock. Little did I know that the bus to the port would be departing any minute. On Saturday, the buses only ran every hour. I decided to trudge on to Parque Castrelos, a half kilometer away, and try to catch the bus there. The yellow arrows pointed down a path that ran along-side of a concrete-contained and tree-lined Rio Legares that weaved its way between apartment buildings.

Upon arriving at Castrelos I noticed a bus stop where the city had posted bus routes and schedules. However, I didn't know what bus I should take to the port area. Not knowing the lay of the land, it was very confusing. So I asked someone who told me to cross the street. When I got there, I learned that I had just missed the bus to the port that passed a block further down the road. So, I started walking in that direction.

Trying to get reliable and understandable information became more than a little frustrating. I resorted to asking every bus driver who stopped which bus to take. Someone told me I should look for bus 12, but there were 12, 12A, and 12B bus lines. I took a seat in the shade and waited and waited. One thing I learned in retirement, especially living in Mexico, is patience. Eventually, a driver told me he could take me close to where I wanted to go. Relieved, I hopped on for the ride.

The bus travelled up hills and down, and weaved through the streets of what appeared to be a modern, well-manicured city. I sat near the driver, and at some point he stopped, motioned for me to get off, and pointed down a street where I should walk. I exited and turned to give him a grateful *muchas gracias*.

The way now went down a gradual hill until I reached a promenade lined by trees and surrounded by hotels and restaurants. Once again, I recognized this place from Google Street View. My hotel sat at the far end, and several cross streets to the left. While walking I made note of the restaurants and bars where I might quench my thirst after checking in. My hotel's exterior appeared just like the pictures. It actually looked a bit elegant. Upon entering though, I found a different story. The tiny lobby had seen better days and needed a serious refurbishment.

I checked in, gathered my backpack, and hiked up the steep and narrow stairs – so narrow that two people would have trouble passing each other, especially with suitcases. I opened the room door to find a dump – the kind of place I might have stayed at when I was a student in the 1960s. It had a double bed that I would later learn needed a new mattress, and a small writing table. The bathroom was small but serviceable, and a window opened to an internal courtyard and didn't close tightly.

After splashing water on my face, combing my hair, and taking another ibuprofen, I went out for a cold beer and snack. I always find it intimidating in a new place when trying to find somewhere to eat. I settled on a welcoming seat in a well-populated bar/café and ordered a beer and a tapa. The late afternoon Sunday crowd sat in couples and families enjoying drinks and light meals. For a few moments, the ibuprofen and alcohol enable me to forget about my injury.

Leaving the restaurant, I turned left and walked back toward the hotel. Feeling better after my snack, I continued past it to the end of the promenade and the start of what appeared to be an older, touristy part of town. It rested on the side of a hill leading down to the water's edge and the port. Small winding streets branched everywhere and begged to be explored. I made mental notes of interesting places to have dinner. Most however were touristy, and priced for a transient clientele.

I find that where the patrons are transient, the food is mediocre and over-priced. After all, the restaurant's business isn't dependent on repeat clientele. Consequently, I prefer to find restaurants where most of the clientele appear to be local. Since I would be in town only overnight, I didn't feel like putting much effort into the endeavor. Besides, I felt too hot and tired to spend much time wandering around the hilly streets. Around the corner from the hotel, I found a bakery with empanadas, and bought several for my walk the next day. Then I returned to the hotel for a shower, power nap and clean change of clothes.

Later that evening, around 8:00, I went in search of dinner. I didn't feel that hungry or like sitting in a fancy place and spending a lot of money. As I wandered, I came upon a little restaurant filled with people - couples, small groups of friends, and families - who all seemed to be having a good time. The sign in front promised seafood. *This is the place*, I told myself. As I entered, I realized that I was probably the only non-local there. I looked around with what must have appeared to be a bewildered expression. A waiter told me to sit anywhere. The tables were a mix of wood and metal tables like the kind you find in so many luncheonettes all over the world. I took a seat near the back where I could observe the scene, ordered a glass of wine, and perused the menu.

The crowd sat with their eyes riveted to several television sets showing a *futbol* game. Occasionally, an animated cheer or an emotional sigh of resignation would emanate from the patrons as the game ebbed and flowed. I expected that I would have another meal of seafood, but the waiters carried plates of what looked like a giant sandwich. So, I stopped one of them to inquire what everybody was eating. "*Hamburguesa*," he informed me. That's the word for hamburger in Spanish. By the looks of the roll, it must have been a giant patty. I didn't need to look at the menu any more. I hadn't had a hamburger in a long, long time. So, I ordered one. When it arrived I feasted on a big, juicy patty and a huge pile of french fries.

Before returning to my room, I asked the desk clerk

whether I could get a taxi at 7:00 the next morning. He assured me it would be no problem. Exhausted, I took an ibuprofen, crawled into bed, found a place where I couldn't feel the springs, and set the alarm for 6:00. Ugh!

At 7:00 the following morning, I brought my pack to the front desk where the desk clerk worked at a computer. We greeted each other commenting on the early hour. I asked him to call me a taxi, and then went outside and sat on the hotel steps in the early morning darkness. The street lights illuminated a deserted promenade to my right. At this hour on a Sunday, there wasn't much competition for taxis, and one showed up after only a few minutes.

Today, September 30, I was walking to Redondela, where the coastal route joins the central route of the Camino Portugues. From there the combined routes continue to Santiago. The day before, I had walked to where the Camino route started to cross Parque Castrelos, and took a bus from there to the port area and my hotel. I had decided to take a taxi back to the Camino at a different point, a landmark, Church of the Peaks, five kilometers beyond Parque Castrelos. I thought that, in the dark, it would be easier to find the yellow arrows at a known landmark.

I think the cab driver thought me to be an odd fare to want to go to that church at that hour. After all, the church was closed. And I found out that he didn't know that the Camino passed right by it. Hardly a vehicle passed on the streets of Galicia's largest city as he weaved his way. In less than 10 minutes he stopped in front of a closed stone structure off a major street. The building sat bathed in darkness.

I found myself standing confused at the bottom of the steps leading to the door of the gated church. All I could identify was a dark, tree-lined street headed downhill to the left of the church, and another well-lit street headed uphill on the right side of the church. The only light came from that street light across the street to the right. It seemed a little eerie and not what I expected to find.

17 WALKING ABOVE THE CLOUDS

I wasn't sure that I had made the right decision to the start the day's walk at this church. It wasn't clear whether I should go up the hill or down. There was no one to ask. My concern mounted as I looked at my map and searched for a yellow arrow or some sign to give me direction. I knew the Camino continued on one of the streets along the church. Starting at this landmark, finding a yellow arrow was not going to be as easy as I thought.

The route came down the major street where the taxi had dropped me off and turned right at the church. So, I started back-tracking up the major street hoping to find an arrow pointing the way, but without luck. So, I went back to the steps.

I needed to make a decision, so I went down the hill in search of an arrow. I wandered around for 15 minutes looking at every wall, telephone pole, and sign post before returning to the church steps. As I approached them, I saw several pilgrims walking up the hill to the right. They must have seen something that I couldn't see. So I followed them up the street, and before I reached the end of the church, a yellow arrow pointed down a narrow street to the right.

As usual, at this time of the day, I started looking for a place to have coffee. I passed a bakery, but they didn't have any. So I kept on walking. Soon the route crossed over a busy street and headed into a residential area. The route led me on a gradual uphill climb and passed a park on the right. It wound its way around the suburban hills overlooking Vigo's harbor, but this morning it hid underneath a layer of low-hanging clouds. I proceeded walking now above the clouds. The sun started to rise ahead and the sky above morphed into a bright blue. Steep streets crossed the route. As I took in my surroundings, I thought about what it must be like to live in a place like this. I could visualize looking out on the city lights at night, and having coffee in the morning above the clouds. I would need a strong pair of legs, and without a lot of practice, I wouldn't want to drive a standard transmission car in this area. I mused that the life-span of car brakes must be on the short side.

The narrow street that I followed proceeded for quite a while through suburban residential neighborhoods. Garage doors backed on to the street, and on the uphill side retaining walls seem to keep the houses from tumbling down the hill. Occasionally, I would pass a farm or vacant lot suspended above the river.

On this Sunday, the Camino walkers had to share the road with weekend bicycle riders. They presented a menace to the walkers. They didn't travel in ones or twos. There were packs of them - entire teams of riders in their team regalia. They were often more interested in carrying on their side-by-side conversations than avoiding hapless pilgrims, many of whom were burdened with their backpacks. It was "walkers beware" until sometime in mid-morning when the cyclists disappeared.

Then, as I walked I heard some women far behind me who were interrupting the morning peacefulness with incessant and loud jabbering. *How could they have so much to talk about, I thought?* As I mentioned in an earlier chapter, I'm a slow walker. So these women kept getting closer and closer and louder and louder. When they came into view, I could see that there were three of them, two middle-age women and an older woman. I could hear by now a distinct Irish accent.

As they pulled up alongside, we exchanged pleasantries. They introduced themselves and told me they were on holiday. The older one, named Mary, seemed to be the instigator for all the talk. They eventually tired of my slow pace. We wished each other a *Buen Camino* and they pulled ahead still talking as they vanished around a bend in the road. I passed them when they stopped to rest. They then passed me when I stopped at a fountain and picnic area on a wooded part of the route to eat the empanada I bought the evening before.

It seems that I wasn't the only one the Irish ladies' presence graced on the Camino. They were sort of notorious. When I reached Redondela, a lot of people spoke of an encounter with them and their non-stop talking. Several days later, I hadn't seen or heard about them for a while. Talking with other pilgrims, I learn that because of Mary's health problems, they needed to end their holiday early and return home.

After stopping at the fountain, I started seeing signs for a café ahead. It was around 10 in the morning, and I still hadn't had a cup of coffee. After another kilometer, a sign to the café, *O Eldo Vello*, pointed up a driveway. I staggered up the incline to find a full-house, and the Irish ladies, who were still talking, enjoying some tea. I got a large café Americano, and took it outside to sit at a free table overlooking the river. It seemed as if someone had removed blinders from my eyes. The clouds that were once below had magically disappeared and I could see the Rande Bridge, a suspension bridge that carries traffic across the Straight of Rande between Vigo and Santiago. The dark blue water, reflecting the sky, danced below it, and the high morning sun illuminated its shimmering spans. It was like being in a helicopter hovering over the bridge, and it seemed so close that I could just reach out and touch it.

Shortly after I resumed my walk, the Camino route diverge to the left off the paved road, and turned into a yellow-soiled dirt road. The sun rose high in the sky, and the temperature rose dramatically with it. I started sweating and put on my Tilly hat to protect my head. I hadn't gone more than a kilometer on the dirt road before I heard someone behind me. As the person overtook me, we recognized each other. He was Tony, one of the "Four Amigos" I met on my first day of walking. His pace was not only faster than mine, but he explained that he outpaced the others in his party too. He liked to walk vigorously, while the other three appreciated a more leisurely pace. He slowed down for me, and we talked for quite a bit for the next several kilometers.

He told me that he and his friends had worked at the same company based in the southern U.S. for many years. They had all moved on to run successful businesses. Now that all of them were retired, they often vacationed together. This was their second Camino. They had planned to dine and sleep well along their walk, and hunted out the best restaurants and hotels wherever they went. As we talked about our experiences so far, I learned they had taken two nights in Baiona, just like me. But, we never saw each other there.

We also had one of those far-ranging conversations that are rare on the Camino -- from our careers, to food and wine, and other travels. I explained about my reason for walking the Camino Portugues, and told him about my accident the day before. At this point, my back began to bother me, and I slowed down even more.

Where the dirt road ended at a paved road, the route made a sharp left turn, and continued down a steep incline of switchbacks. I was glad I had my walking poles to brake my descent. I found going downhill much harder than going up. I had my feet extended at a weird angle, my knees were taking most of my weight, and my quads were in pain and burned as they broke my momentum downwards. The pain in my back kept getting worse. Even going from side to side put stress on the outsides of my feet, and compensating for my back threw off my balance.

I needed a rest and after a half kilometer at a steep angle, the road leveled off for a few hundred meters before coming to a four corners called Cedeira. We sat at a picnic table, next to a bus stop, downhill from a church and waited for Tony's friends. Shortly afterwards, the woman I had met on my way to lunch on the first day of walking, Judy, sauntered up to join us. She was married to the slow poke of the group, Bob. The fourth member of the party, Nikki, was married to a doctor back in the states who couldn't take the time off to walk with them.

Judy was searching for a bathroom, and had no idea how far back Bob and Nikki were. I wanted to start walking again before I got too stiff. During my talks with Tony he told me they were staying at a hotel in Padron, the last stop before Santiago, called Chef Rivera. There is a restaurant in the hotel with a good reputation. I told him that I too had a reservation there the same night. We had chosen it for the same reason, the food. Before we parted, we made a date for all of us to have dinner together in Padron four days hence.

18 LOST AGAIN

I picked up my walking poles and started in the direction of Redondela. The landscape had changed. I was now walking in a valley. Farms gently stretched out toward the Rego des Maceiras, a small river, a kilometer or two somewhere over the horizon to my right. As I walked by well-kept farm houses and green fields and dodged an occasional car, I became engrossed in my wandering thoughts.

In the process, I absent-mindedly shuffled past a yellow arrow pointing down a narrow farm road. After a bit, I thought it curious that I hadn't seen any arrows for a while. Then over a rise, I saw the highway ahead. For sure, I thought, there would be an arrow at that intersection. But when I got to the highway I didn't see any. I looked to the right and left and across the road. I realized that I must have missed an arrow.

I started thinking that I had lost my mind. This was the second boondoggle in one day. Once again, but now in a weary state, I would need to expend unnecessary energy to walk an extra distance. When you're walking with other people, everyone helps each other stay on the route. Walking alone, and without a GPS, I couldn't rely on anything or anyone else to help find the correct way. I vowed to pay more attention.

I found myself in a quandary about which way to walk. I knew that Redondela was close. The midday sun blazed now and the highway pavement intensified the oven-like temperatures. I started walking downhill to the right. There were only a few intersections, but I needed to stop and question myself at each of them. I continued for another kilometer around a bend, and then I could see the cut-off for Redondela ahead. I passed a street on my right, and saw some pilgrims walking down it. That is where I should have come out.

I could see the Irish ladies walking down the road to the right. As they approached, I could hear them talking – even over the noise of the traffic. I stood and waited to greet them. A difference of opinion arose between them regarding where to cross the highway, and where the Camino continued. I could see the town on the other side of the highway and the river it fronted. It didn't matter to me where the arrows were. I crossed the highway, walked across a restaurant parking lot, through a tunnel, over a bridge, and into the center of Redondela. Between the missteps at the beginning and end of my walk I had probably added 2-3 kilometers to my day.

The night before in Vigo, I had rehearsed the next day's route. Looking at a map, it seemed as though it would be easy to find the alburgue. I was standing at a roundabout in the center of town. A park with a court house sat at the far end of a grassy area to my left, and a railroad trestle passed over my head. This town teemed with pilgrims. There were more of them walking around here than I had seen in one place since starting my Camino.

Redondela is the convergence of the inland and coastal routes of the Camino Portugues. The inland route is the most widely traveled. I walked the less-traveled coastal route. When I planned my Camino, I read about the inland route on the forums. Many people complained about cobblestones. The street where I live in Mexico has cobblestones, as do many in the surrounding area. Cobblestones are difficult to navigate when walking to the grocery store, and even harder when walking home after a few drinks. Where I live they are a common cause of sprained ankles, broken wrists, and cracked teeth. I had no interest in dealing with kilometers of them on my Camino.

At this point, I started looking for a private albergue called *A Conserveira* on Rua Pai Crespo. It was supposed to be the second street crossing my path. At that intersection, a narrow street drowned in shadows extended to my right and left. I walked to the left for a long block. The street numbers weren't right. I later learned that while this street looked like an extension of Pia Crespo, the street names changed at the previous intersection. So I reversed my direction, and at the trestle, I saw the sign for Pia Crespo. I proceeded walking and looking for the building number of the albergue. I must have missed it and walked to the end in frustration. Once again, I turned around and finally spotted the non-descript door to A Conserveira. It was so plain it could have been a dentist office.

After ringing a bell at the door, a young lady let me in and registered me. Before taking me to my bunk, she showed me around the facility, told me the rules, and retrieved my backpack. Because of my hip, I had requested a lower bunk. She left after showing me where to store my pack and where to find a blanket if I needed one. A stocky man lay in the top bunk fixated on his cell phone to whom I introduced myself. His name was Ernst, and he hailed from Bavaria, he told me adamantly - not Germany, but Bavaria. Ernst appeared to be in his mid to late fifties, and was traveling with four middle aged women. I'm not sure if he started the Camino with them, or picked them up along the way.

I had never stayed in a mixed dormitory style albergue before. It had a large room that housed about 40 people, divided by thin wooden walls into smaller quarters of two or four bunks. Each quarter had curtains to separate it from a center aisle. Every bunk had a small reading light and outlet to charge electrical devices, as well as a lockable half locker. There were separate wash rooms. Everything looked clean and new.

Pilgrims sat and reclined in their bunks napping, reading or checking messages on their cell phones. Others, fresh off the trail, headed to the washroom to shower and clean up. For so many people in the room, the quietness surprised me. No one raised their voice. Everyone talked in hushed tones.

I stowed some of my things before splashing my face

with water, and heading out for a bite to eat. It must have been around 2 p.m. Once again, I walked the streets looking for a place and settled on a restaurant called Samoa. I couldn't even speculate where the name came from, but the décor and food were not reminiscent of the South Pacific. The room was large, and the tables and multi-colored chairs gave it the feel of a luncheonette. It had a very Spanish menu. I didn't spy anyone that looked like a pilgrim. Rather, the clientele appeared to be locals, families and couples, out for their Sunday, midday meals.

I like busy restaurants, where locals choose to eat, and Samoa had an interesting weekend menu filled with the customary Galician standards. As usual, I chose from the weekend menu. There was a wide variety of choices, but I chose the *gambas al ajillo* (shrimp in garlic) for the first course, and *entrecote* al roquefort (steak with a roquefort sauce) for the second course. The meal included wine, and when I finished, I had consumed a few glasses.

By then, it was late afternoon, and I didn't feel like exploring the town. So I retired back to the albergue, and took an ibuprofen for my back. I then plugged in my cell phone, took out my tablet, and climbed into my bunk and reclined. *Whoa! What a great mattress.* It was the best of the trip so far. For the first time in a couple days, I put my earphones on, closed my eyes and listened to music. The forty other people in the albergue vanished from my consciousness, as did the pain in my back.

The next morning, the alarm on my cell phone woke me up, and I rushed to turn it off hoping I hadn't woken anyone. The room was dark except for a soft night light and the lights from the outside hallway that led to the washrooms. I could hear a stirring in the room as I lay in bed stretching and wiggling my toes. The mattress felt so comfortable I didn't want to get up. After a few minutes, I quietly slipped out of my bunk and tip-toed to the washroom.

I had packed my backpack the night before and laid out any clothes I would need in the morning. Returning to my bunk, I grabbed my footwear and went into the well-lit reception area to sit and go through my morning foot preparation ritual. I found several other early risers making their breakfast and preparing to leave. When ready, I returned to the dormitory for my pack and left it behind the unattended front desk.

I shut the albergue door behind me, turned to the left and a block later came to an intersection with several cafes. I went into the Cafeteria Farola where I had breakfast, bought food for the walk, and had my credencial stamped.

It was Monday, October 1. I planned to walk about 20 kilometers to Pontevedra, a city with a population of about 83,000. I would be taking another day of rest there before my final three day push to Santiago. The way would be varied – country farm roads, dangerous highways, and paths through the woods. 20 kilometers would be pushing the upper limits of my abilities, especially now because of my back. Nevertheless, aside from taking a bus or a day of rest, I didn't really have an option. Changing my accommodations and the schedule of my baggage pick-ups would have been a logistical nightmare. At any rate, I looked forward to the day's walk, and happy that there were only four more days of walking.

19 THE BEAR WENT OVER THE MOUNTAIN

At this point in the story, I should share a few of my observations about walking the Camino. I had walked four days on a trail of varying difficulty. So far, I had been lucky with the weather. There had been no rain. For the most part, the skies had been bright blue. The mornings had been crisp and great for walking; the afternoons had been quite warm, and the evenings pleasant. The scenery had changed from coastal to suburban to rural, and the food had been good. Except for my back, I was relatively pain-free. My foot preparation worked well. I had not experienced a blister yet.

I'm not sure how to describe how I felt. While on the one hand, I was pumped up and enthusiastic about meeting the challenges each day brought, on the other, I started feeling a kind of mental fatigue. Many of the accounts I've read and people I've talked with about the Camino, build high expectations and gloss over the reality of getting up each day, walking for mile upon mile, and doing it again the next day and the next, etc. It's a grind. It takes a toll on your body, and yes, your spirit too. I started to question why I even bothered to do the Camino. When I got home, people would ask me if I had a good time.

My answer still is: *"I wouldn't call it a good time. It was a grind. It was difficult and challenging, but it was worth it."*

As soon as I left the café and started walking, any mental fatigue I experienced started to vanish. There's something invigorating about walking in the early morning before the sun has risen. The air is crisp, and there is a hushed silence, except for the birds coming to life. Any stiffness from the day and night before begins to melt away, and life takes on a rhythm one step at a time.

The Camino route headed north on a street across from the café until it got to the highway and a crosswalk. Darkness still hovered above, but the street lights helped illuminate the way. After crossing, the yellow arrows pointed down a side street lined with industrial buildings until gradually heading uphill into a residential area. The narrow road continued to climb until, after walking for fifteen minutes, the paved road dead-ended at a farm house, and a gravel road continued uphill to the left.

I found it quite peaceful to be walking alone this morning in a now rural area. I could hear the birds chirping in the trees. On occasion, a car or truck would pass out-of-sight on Highway 550 a few hundred meters up the hill where it headed north out of Redondela. My sneakers shuffling on the gravel road and the planting of my walking poles were the only other sounds I heard.

Every noise in this bucolic place seemed to carry. The road then passed by several fields lined with rock walls.

As I neared the top of an incline, I stopped. Loud singing broke the peace of the morning. There were people singing on the road behind me. They weren't singing hiking, camping, or marching songs. No, they were singing a song by Jim Morrison and The Doors from the early 1970s. I thought it a weird song to be singing so early in the morning. It might have been welcome if they only had better voices! You might expect the choice of that song after a few drinks in the evening. But, who am I to judge? They may have gotten an early start on the day and spiked their coffee with brandy.

As the singers appeared from around a bend in the road, I could see two men briskly approaching with an animated walk. They raised their walking poles as they sang at the top of their lungs. The taller of the men had an athletic build, and the smaller, stocky one, sported a big bushy mustache. When they passed they greeted me in Italian. I answered, "Buen Camino," in Spanish and "have a fun day" in English They marched off still singing, and left me pondering the weirdest and most unusual event of my Camino.

The route took me across the highway and through several farmland intersections before the arrows pointed me up a hill and into the woods. At the top of a rise, Ernst from Bavaria and the albergue passed me with his harem of four women. We exchanged greetings, and they rapidly disappeared down the wooded track ahead of me at a pace I couldn't attempt to match.

The sun had risen, but the temperature remained cool. I walked through the woods on a well-worn dirt road. Power lines kept creeping in and out of sight on my left, and I alternately passed farms separated by rock walls and overgrown fields that had become lightly wooded areas. I was relieved to finally be walking in the woods, and leaving the suburban sprawl of the Vigo area behind me. Although I could have avoided Vigo by taking the more rural inland route, I would have missed the days of walking along the ocean.

However, there were many more pilgrims on the path now than I had experienced before Redondela. I realized that many more people must travel the inland route of the Camino Portugues than the coastal route. At the time, I imagined that this is what much of the final 100 kilometers of the Camino Frances must be like from Sarria to Santiago. But since returning, I learned that the route from Sarria is much more crowded than what I experienced.

On this beautiful morning, I didn't see or hear the Irish ladies, and the Italians must have been far ahead out of hearing range. People talked in hushed tones and passed me quietly. Most appeared contemplative. After all, it was still early in the morning at a time when conversation doesn't often come easily.

The path in the woods rose gradually for several kilometers, crossing a road, and passing a few more farms before starting a steep descent to the town of Arcade and the Verdugo River. The path diverted onto a shaded paved two-lane road and continued downhill to the highway and a rest stop where I arrived around 9:00.

In a small picnic area along the highway, a family had set up a pop-up tent with refreshments. They sold coffee, soft drinks, and pastries, as well as souvenirs to an eager group of pilgrims that had queued up. The two Italians were finishing their snack when I arrived and left quickly. The Bavarians were nowhere to be seen. I bought coffee and a pastry, and had my credencial stamped before finding an empty plastic chair in which to rest.

Cars on the highway roared past. The peace of the woods seemed so far away from this place. Nevertheless, I observed a mixed group of people from all over the world who were grateful for the services the family provided and the opportunity to rest. I only spent about 15 minutes, before slinging my daypack on my back, and stiffly started walking up the highway's shoulder. After 100 meters the shoulder disappeared. The highway was a four-lane road that, at this point, climbed a pretty steep grade to a crest one-half kilometer away. Trucks zoomed treacherously close as groups of pilgrims trudged toward the top.

At the crest of the hill, I had a downhill view to the center of Arcade and the Verdugo River about a kilometer away. The Camino route went right through the center of town. Cafes along this route were busy serving pilgrims. Crowds filled the sidewalk tables and overflowed out the doors. Since I already had my mid-morning snack a little while before, I strolled by the madness feeling fortunate I didn't need to stand in line. As I walked, the Bavarians were sitting at a table. I think they were drinking beers. I waved and Ernst waved back.

The café street eventually took me to the Ponte

Sampaio, a one-way stone bridge over the Verdugo built by the Romans, and the scene of an important battle in the Peninsular Wars in 1809.

On the other side of the river, the path led up steep streets lined with stone faced houses. The yellow arrows led to a country lane that dead-ended at an intersection. There the Camino continued down a path, into the woods and over another stream, Rio Ullo. From this point, the path climbed and descended for several kilometers.

For the first several hundred meters, rain had washed out the path requiring careful navigation over and around exposed rocks and boulders. Walking became easier after the washed out section. The path passed a wine processing plant on the left then climbed another hill with verdant trees and fields on the uphill side and harvested vineyards downhill.

Once again, I found myself walking in the woods. It felt like new-growth forest, populated by trees that popped up on land previously cleared. The trail had more people on it, and I never felt alone. The path continued uphill and down. As I walked, I fell into a numbing mindlessness and started to sing to myself a song from childhood:

The bear went over the mountain
The bear went over the mountain
The bear went over the mountain
To see what he could see

He saw another mountain
He saw another mountain
He saw another mountain

So what do you think he did?

He climbed another mountain...

You get it!

After several kilometers, at a crossroad, another family served snacks and drinks under a tent in the shade. I stopped, bought some water, and a croissant, and after taking off my pack, sat in a folding chair to rest. The leaves in this place had started to turn, and the sun started to feel hot. I didn't check the time, but my body told me I was starting to get tired.

After the rest stop, the path went uphill once more before it started its descent on a gravel road. At times the going got steep and slippery, and I depended on my walking poles quite a bit to brake myself and keep my balance. I didn't realize it at the time that this would be the last big downhill for the day. On the way down, I struck up a conversation with a couple from somewhere in the Midwest. We got around to talking about unusual topics such as the stock market and American politics. Most of the time, I stay away from such topics since they can be divisive, nothing is ever solved, and most of the time, someone gets offended or angry. That didn't happen in our conversation, and we agreed that it had been a nice change to have someone with whom to talk.

At the bottom of the hill, the way passed between several houses and a café, and continued down a path constructed of hard-packed gravel, and into the woods again. I felt relieved that the terrain here was fairly level.

Maybe, I thought, it would be better for my back. But while I tried to concentrate on other things, my back would bother me for the next 6 kilometers to Pontevedra. The trees hung low arching over the trail providing shade, cool air, and relief from the midday sun. After a short stretch, the path opened to fields and vineyards for a kilometer or two before joining the highway at the chapel of Santa Marta.

Just before the chapel, I passed a small winery. An organized tour had just entered for lunch and a tasting. I followed them in to check out the place. We entered a tasting room with yellow painted walls where a long, aged wooden table had been set for the group's lunch.

The owner told me that Spain has a special license for farmers who grow their own grapes. It allows them to sell on their premises. In a former life, I had been a winemaker, and had owned a small winery. Although I didn't grow my own grapes, my license allowed me to sell retail on the premises and wholesale to stores and restaurants. I got a chance to ask a few questions and see his production and storage areas. I would have liked to have talked with the owner at length, but he was busy with the group, and I needed to continue.

Down the highway, a few hundred meters to the left came another decision point. From Santa Marta there are two routes into Pontevedra, both about 4 kilometers long.

20 PONTEVEDRA

A big bulletin board size map stood on the corner. It showed one route relatively straight that followed the highway into Pontevedra, and another squiggly route that followed the Rio Tomeza. Both routes converged several hundred meters south of Pontevedra's railroad station near a municipal albergue.

I'm glad the Camino provided an alternative because I didn't want to be walking again along a highway in the midday heat with cars and trucks speeding by. It had been pleasant to walk for most of the day in the woods or on country roads passing farms and vineyards. So, I turned left down a farm road until a sign ushered me down a path and into the refreshing shade of the trees lining Rio Tomeza. The river, at this point, little more than a trickling stream, meandered on and on for several kilometers.

The path occasionally peaked out of the woods to follow a farm road, and then sneaked back in. At one juncture, a wooden shelter with benches sat bathed in the shadows of several large trees. Numerous pilgrims rested in the shade, drinking water, eating a snack, checking their equipment, and exchanging stories. Those of us staying in Pontevedra knew that the day's walk would be ending in only 1-2 kilometers, and while we were weary and hot, the mood seemed upbeat.

The path then wandered under several highways. At one point, I rounded a corner to find the "Four Amigos" in a small grassy glen just off the trail to the right. They were enjoying a gourmet lunch of goodies they had scavenged from groceries and bakeries along the way. As I approached them to say hello, they asked me if I'd like to join them.

"Come on," they implored, "we just opened a can of sardines, and there's olives, and salami, and some nice fresh crusty bread."

I was tempted to accept their offer, and thought long and hard. After all, I would have liked to get to know them better. But, they were sitting on the ground and I really needed a better place to sit. Since my hip replacement, it had been difficult to get to the ground or floor and even harder to get up. In addition, my legs and back were feeling very tired, and I could feel myself starting to stoop forward as I walked. That exacerbated the pain from my injury. I feared that if I stopped for a while, it would be extremely difficult to carry on. In addition, I was anxious to get to the hotel before the afternoon sun hit its peak. We affirmed our dinner date in Padron in three days, and I continued on my way.

The path along the river emerged at a railroad bridge.

Paper and painted signs covered the large white stones of the bridge abutment. A yellow arrow pointed the way to the left. The route passed a private albergue, then the municipal albergue. At the train station I came to a multi-cornered intersection that, at first glance, I couldn't decipher.

Walking into a strange city poses challenges that are resolved easier when traveling by car. With little effort, a driver can rectify a wrong turn in a car by turning around or going around a block. When on foot, you can walk for half a kilometer before realizing your folly. At the end of the day, being hot and tired, this can be quite disturbing. After all, you know you are so close to your destination. I had already made several mistakes during my Camino, including two the day before, and I was determined not to make another.

Standing at that intersection, I felt like being a contestant on "The Price is Right." If I choose the right door, I win the grand prize of making it "effortlessly" to my destination. Choose the wrong door, and I might be in for a long afternoon. It took me a while to find a yellow arrow, and then decipher my cryptic map.

Downtown Pontevedra is a modern and clean city, but as with many gentrified older city centers, it suffers from a maze of streets left from generations ago. I had a reservation at the Hotel Madrid in a "new" section, a block or two from the historical district. I tried navigating the maze of streets. After asking directions several times, I was relieved to be at the bottom of the steps leading to a sparse, but modern lobby. After checking in, I felt more relieved when I learned that the hotel had an elevator I could take to my third-floor air conditioned room.

After cleaning myself up and taking a short nap, I consulted Google Maps for the nearest laundromat. I had no intention of doing laundry that afternoon, but I wanted to go out to explore and find a snack. Right around the corner I saw a laundry drop-off. The place had bags filled with clothes stacked everywhere either waiting to be cleaned or picked up. The woman behind the counter confirmed what I thought. They would not be able to have my clothes ready in 24 hours.

So, I turned and started walking in the opposite direction toward a self-service establishment. On Google Maps, It appeared to be a half kilometer down a busy street. On the way, I also hoped to find a café where I could get a tapa and beer for a snack. About half way to the laundromat, I stopped at Bar Skala at the end of an overpass. There were only a few people there having coffee and checking their cell phones. I took an outside table in the shade, and surveyed the other customers and traffic on the street. It felt good to get off my feet and rest my back. I looked forward to a day of rest, and started making a plan for the next day.

After having several beers and a snack, I stood up to pay the waitress who had been ignoring me for most of my visit, and the alcohol went right to my head. Rather than continuing to the laundromat, I walked back toward the hotel and the historic district.

In the late 1990s, Pontevedra banned most vehicle traffic from the streets in the historic district. Today, it's possible to walk almost anywhere without encountering a car or truck. Today, historic buildings, parks, residences, modern stores of all types, sidewalk cafes and restaurants line the streets.

Just before getting to my hotel, I turned right up a street with a gentle grade. The street ended at the Children's Fountain where I spotted a yellow arrow. With nothing else to do, I decided to follow it. The way followed a shopping street and passed through what seemed to be an endless succession of plazas, government buildings and churches, including the Pilgrims Chapel. I decided to wait until the next day to go in. After exploring the back streets for an hour, I stopped in a café, ordered a glass of wine, and munched on some chips before heading to the hotel for a nap before dinner.

Dinner turned out to be an interesting experience. To the side of the Pilgrims Chapel, I found a rather full restaurant, Sidreria Montañes, with an appealing menu. It sat a few steps up and shared an outdoor patio with another restaurant. A *sidreria* is a place where they serve cider, for which Galicia is famous. However, a cold Albariño interested me more than a sweet cider. As I sat and waited for my wine, street lights on a plaza behind the church cast a yellow glow over everything.

I noticed several neighboring tables with a strange contraption on them. I watched as customers served themselves cider from it.

The traditional way to serve cider in Galicia is to hold the bottle high above a wide-mouth glass and pour a small portion. In the process the cider gets aerated. The technique is called *escanciar un culín* (also *echar un culín*), and gives the cider a sparkling taste. The strange table-top contraption I saw emulated the hand-poured method. The user places a tube from the machine in the cider bottle, and puts a glass at the other end. When you push a button, a pump draws the cider into the machine where it is measured, chilled, and aerated. Full of fizz, it's poured into the glass. Later in my trip, I did experience cider, but I regretted not ever having it served this way.

I struck up a conversation with some Americans at the table next to mine about the food and what they were eating. I forget what I ordered, but while waiting for my meal, I saw the Italian crooners from early in the morning. I went over to say hello, but it took them a while to remember me. I reminded them about their singing Jim Morrison songs and big smiles broke out on their faces. We wished each other well, and I returned to my table.

As I finished my meal, the night started to feel a little nippy. It was a relief to know that I didn't have to walk in the morning. The day off would give my feet and back a welcome rest, and I looked forward to sleeping a little later too.

When you're used to getting up at 6:00 in the morning, 7:00 seems late. I decided to skip my morning foot prep, and dressed for the day. From the day before, I remembered a café, El Dulce de Leche, around the corner to the left after leaving the hotel. At 8:00 in the morning, it hummed with activity. People were reading their newspapers and checking their cell phones before going to work. I ordered my usual breakfast and sat for a while reviewing my plan for the day.

Returning to the room, I gathered dirty clothes to take to the laundromat. It felt good to be stretching my legs again as I walked a peaceful half kilometer to the laundromat. I spotted a little café around the corner where I partook of my second and third cups of coffee and wrote my email journal while the clothes washed and then dried.

The rest of the day, I explored the historic district, stopping to get my credencial stamped at the Pilgrims Chapel, the floor of which is laid out like a scallop shell. While walking, I happened upon the Renaissance style Basilica of St. Mary Major where I picked up another stamp for my credencial. Then, as I walked back toward the hotel, I saw a café with a sign that said "*Vermuteria*," a place where vermouth is served.

In my research for my trip to Spain, I kept finding references about vermouth. Vermouth is a fortified spiced red or white wine. Most Americans know the red as an ingredient in Manhattans, and the white as an ingredient in Martinis. Instead of imbibing a beer or wine in the late afternoon, the Spanish drink it as an aperitif served on ice by itself. It is popular in Galicia, but Spaniards serve it all over the country. There are some large producers, but most are regional, and it's not unusual to find homemade vermouth at some establishments. There are as many recipes as there are vermouth makers.

I came back to the "vermuteria" later in the afternoon to try the wine for the first time. The wine was sweet but tasted flavored with savory herbs. The usual garnish for white is a piece of lemon, and a piece of orange for the red. From that time forward, I made vermouth part of my late afternoon cocktail hours as I travelled around Spain.

Dinnertime found me wandering the streets again trying to find a place to eat. I found a little narrow street, Rua Figueroa hopping with activity and several restaurants with outside tables. I sat at a place busy with locals and tourists. As I sat, I caught a conversation from a neighboring table that the owner had previously run one of the other restaurants on the street, and recently bought this one. Then, as I waited for my check, I heard people at another table talking with a Boston accent, and stopped to talk with them for a few minutes. They were on a guided tour, not walking the Camino.

The next day would be a challenge, so I retired to my hotel. There would be no sleeping "late" the next morning.

PART 3

DISCOVERY

21 WEARINESS OF THE SOLO WALKER

The next morning, the desk clerk directed me to leave my pack next to the couch in the lobby. I thanked him, pushed the heavy glass doors open, and walked down the stairs to the street. I looked across the street at the plaza and then up at the still starlit sky. Today promised to be another sunny and cloudless day.

For breakfast, I had two choices right in the neighborhood. To the left, I could return to the place I had had breakfast yesterday, El Dulce de Leche. To my right, directly around the corner I had seen a smaller *panaderia* called Acuña with tables. Either way, I'd be one block from the Children's Fountain where I'd need to pick-up the Camino route.

I chose Acuña because I hadn't tried it yet. A mix of people sat at plastic-topped tables huddled over their coffee and pastry. Half the customers were women and that made this place different from other breakfast cafes I had been to. Many of them were busy on their cell phones. This made another departure from my early hour experiences at cafes where most, if not all, the customers were men who were reading newspapers. I ordered my usual breakfast and took it to a table in the back where I could observe people coming and going.

I sat and contemplated my walk for the day. This day, Wednesday, October 3, began a three day push to Santiago walking at least 20 kilometers each day. Today, I would be walking to Caldas de Reyes, which means "cauldron of the kings" in English. The town is known for its hot springs. The one day of rest had done wonders for my feet and back. So, after tightening my laces one more time, I started on my way.

The Camino route winds its way through Pontevedra's historic district passing by the Pilgrims Chapel, until it reaches the Rio Lerez at the Burgos Bridge, built in the 12th century. From there, it proceeds uphill on a narrow residential street and through the suburbs of Pontevedra. After a kilometer the houses became further apart and I began to pass small farms. The road continued up a gradual incline following, and then passing under railroad tracks, and through a little town.

Shortly after that, the incline got steeper and the road passed by the Iglesia Santa Maria Alba, part of a complex of what appeared to be religious buildings. The complex was closed and I didn't see a soul anywhere. Looking to the left, while standing on the road, I saw a separate and eerie gated area filled with what looked like a group of attached crypts. It reminded me of a grotesque self-storage area, built out of stone, to store human remains for centuries.

A few kilometers ahead, the route crossed the railroad tracks again and started an ascent to the village of San Amaro and a welcomed coffee break. At that point, I had walked about 8 kilometers. I still had about 12 kilometers more to go.

By that time in my Camino, I didn't think about the difference in the distances I covered on the pilgrimage from the distances when I trained during the summer. To do so, probably would have made it difficult to continue. I had started my Camino only one week earlier from A Guarda. Every day consisted of putting one foot before the other until I reached my daily goal. That's not to say that I didn't enjoy the countryside through which I walked or the observations I made about other pilgrims and interesting things along the way.

The act of walking a Camino is deliberate, especially if you walk it alone. It has to be because there are always physical or mental obstacles you have to overcome. If you don't like being by yourself, especially for long periods of time, I would not suggest walking a Camino. It also helps if you're goal oriented.

No one ever asks what you think about while you're walking hour after hour with only the thoughts in your head. And you do talk to yourself. You sing songs long-forgotten that suddenly pop into your head…sometimes out loud, sometimes under your breath, sometimes in your mind. You entertain yourself by counting steps or twirling your walking poles. You plan your next day. You think about your next meal. You long for the day's walk to be over.

Some days, I found it easier to reach my daily goal than others. But the days were starting to be a blur, and doubts about why I decided to put myself through this experience became more frequent. These feelings tended to occur toward the end of each day. By that time, I felt hot and weary, and the thoughts of completing the day's walk were consuming. "*Just keep walking. It's only a little bit further. You can do it*," I would cheer myself on.

There were times when I thought about whether I should continue my Camino, especially when my back got sore. There are so many things that could happen that could end your Camino. Severe blisters, shin splints, food poisoning, a virus, or even a dog bite would be a temporary setback. After some rest and remediation, you could start walking again. If a car hit you, or you broke a leg, your walk would be over. At my age, you might have to worry about a heart attack, stroke, respiratory problems, or some other chronic ailment.

Since hurting my back, my body did well for the first 15 kilometers, but the last few were getting more and more difficult to complete. Only continuous unbearable pain or the risk of further injury could turn me back, but I found that a night's rest patched me up sufficiently to continue the next day.

I had started out to walk a Camino to Santiago, and I became determined to finish it. I think about those who walk from France to Santiago, and marvel at the grit and determination it takes to complete that trip. I had chosen a shorter, "easier" walk for reasons I've explained. That doesn't diminish the grit and determination it takes to walk 100 plus kilometers of any of the Caminos.

***

Pousada do Peregrino stood where the walking path entered the village of San Amaro. A courtyard lined with picnic tables guarded the entrance to the *pousada*. Pilgrims filled the place enjoying a break. Knapsacks, walking poles and day packs littered the ground. I entered the building with my daypack still on which made it difficult to navigate a narrow hallway. It opened to a crowded room with more tables and a coffee bar. I left my poles and daypack at the end of a long table, and tried to figure out which line to stand on to place my order. Everyone jockeyed for position. Eventually, I reached the bar, ordered coffee and a snack, and returned to my equipment.

As I waited for the coffee to cool, I surveyed the people in the room to see if I knew anyone. There were people I recognized who had passed me that day. I thought about where all the rest of these people might come from

I tried to stretch my feet out and rest them on my heels. It sounds kind of strange, but it was the next best thing for my feet to either putting them up or lying down. I had found in my training that taking all the weight off the soles and balls of my feet for a few minutes did wonders when I stood up again.

Leaving the pousada, I took a sharp right turn and headed downhill. After a kilometer, the route leveled out and wandered through farm roads, little villages, and vineyards for many kilometers. There were still a few grapes in the vineyards. Once in a while I'd pass a farmer tending his grapes. I stopped to talk with one about his work and what types of grapes he grew. But, I had trouble understanding the Galician dialect which is infused with a lot of Portuguese. Added to that, there are many varieties of grapes and they are often called different names in different countries or even regions of the same country. While I recognized some names in our conversation, I was clueless about others he mentioned.

22 SO THIS IS WHAT IT"S ALL ABOUT

Around two o'clock, with my back hurting and leaning slightly to the right, I found myself stumbling into Calda de Reis along a shady, narrow stretch of N-550. The stone-faced buildings hugged a narrow sidewalk, and cars wizzed by too close for comfort. A river flows through Caldas, and the highway crossed it at a lush green park to the right. An interesting looking restaurant on the far side of the bridge opened to the park and river. I made a mental note to come back and try it for dinner.

After crossing the bridge, a yellow arrow pointed down a cobblestone walking street that I followed until it met the first major cross street. I turned left and headed a few hundred meters to my lodgings for the evening, Hotel Sena.

The Hotel Sena turned out to be the social highlight of my Camino. To this point, I hadn't had much social interaction, except for occasional conversations. But, I had not yet sat down to have dinner or drinks with other pilgrims. It was a dynamic missing from my journey. I pondered whether it was more common when you stay in albergues all the time.

After checking in, I dropped my pack in my second floor air-conditioned room and put on a pair of sandals. Then, I headed downstairs for the outside patio and a beer. A few people were eating their midday meal as I let the cold brew chill my throat. The first sip of beer is always the best, especially when the weather is hot. With my feet stretched out, a feeling of satisfaction swept over me. I had walked 20 kilometers, and I felt as though I didn't have a care until the next morning.

Hotel Sena has a pool, so after my beer I went exploring the property. An English-speaking couple sat on the edge of the pool in their bathing suits dangling their feet in the water. I recognized them from the day's walk, and stopped to talk with them for a minute. "Take your shoes off," they suggested. "The water's too cold to swim but it feels great on your feet."

I took them up on their suggestion. They were right. The chill from the water almost hurt as it cooled the blood that ran up my legs. It gave me a chill. They were from Florida and had walked from the Portuguese border on the inland route and were looking forward to the end of their pilgrimage. We were only two days from Santiago. We could all start to feel the excitement of getting there.

I left them after fifteen minutes and went to my room for a nap and a shower. When I came down later, it was still too early to go for dinner. So, I ordered a glass of Albariño and watched as people from the Camino filtered in. Three women sat directly in front of me, and two couples I had met in Pontevedra sat to my left. One of them lived in New Jersey and the other in Rhode Island. The men were brothers and of Portuguese decent. The couples had decided to combine a visit to their homeland with a Camino that would allow them time to bond.

I'm not sure how it got started, but I inserted myself into the conversation of the three women. After talking across tables for a few minutes, they invited me to join them. They were having a reunion of sorts. They were long-time friends, who lived far apart – California, Oregon, and Ohio - but often vacationed together. They weren't stopping their pilgrimage at Santiago, but would be extending it a few days to Fisterra at the Atlantic Ocean. When the topic of dinner came up, I scrapped plans to eat at the restaurant on the river, and opted to continue the conversation.

We ordered dinner, and as we were finishing, the two brothers were getting drunk on some rather potent alcoholic beverage they had bought in Portugal. The noise level went up considerably as they started singing and passing their bottle around the dining room. As we headed to our rooms, we said goodbye, not expecting to see each other again as often happens on the Camino.

I took an ibuprofen and lay down in bed, warmed by the way the evening had progressed, but worried about my back. I wasn't sure I could make it all the way to Santiago. I had two days of 20 plus kilometers of walking left.

23 IT'S ALL DOWNHILL FROM HERE

The next morning, I was one of the first people to stop into the hotel's café. One man sat in the corner reading the morning's newspaper. At this hour, I didn't expect to see anyone from the night before. I couldn't help but think that the Portuguese-Americans were having a tough time opening their eyes after finishing the bottle of who-knows-what the night before. And, I can't imagine how long it would take three women to prepare for the day while sharing one bathroom.

When I stepped outside, the air had an unusual bite. It seemed colder than previous mornings, and a chill penetrated my fleece vest and light-weight tee shirt. My feelings were confirmed as I briskly walked under a sign flashing the time and temperature: "7:15 – 5° " (45 degrees F). Even though I knew that I would be warm after a few minutes, I felt grateful that there was no breeze.

Today, Thursday, October 4, I'd be walking to Padron, about 20 kilometers north. Padron was the last stop before

Santiago. According to my guide book, the Camino would rise for 5.5 kilometers to a town called Carracedo, and then descend gradually for the next 15 kilometers to Padron. My back felt a little sore as I walked to the cross street where the Camino route continued. I turned left and headed north, over a small bridge to a junction with the highway. A few hundred meters up the highway, the route started down a narrow street. At the bottom of the hill, the street became a gravel path that followed power lines to Carracedo.

When I trained, I would often walk 5 kilometers on the carretera from my house in Mexico to the town of Chapala. The walk always seemed to take me one-hour and ten minutes. It didn't matter if I thought I walked fast or slow; or whether I stopped to take a break or not. It always took me one-hour and ten minutes. So as I started down the gravel path, I figured that it would take me more or less one-hour and ten minutes until a coffee break in Carracedo, somewhere around 8:45.

It didn't take too long before people started passing me as usual - two men walking together, then three, then a group of 20-somethings. Every time I'd hear the clicking of their walking poles on the gravel behind me, it seemed fruitless to try to speed up.

I felt grateful that the level path made walking easy. A mist hung over the trees beyond the power lines. The fields of the farms along the way were also bathed in a mist that the made the dew on the green glisten in the encroaching sun. After a while, the path started to rise, ending in a steep upgrade before spilling out next to a hilltop field at the crest. Walking up a cobblestone stretch to two stone pillars at the end made me think of the yellow brick road. A short jog to the left took me to the highway and Café Bar Esperon housed in an unassuming yellow building. I followed two pilgrims to the door. My watch registered 8:45.

Inside, I discovered a frenzy of activity. Pilgrims packed the place wall-to-wall. Backpacks and walking poles cluttered the floor and leaned against the wall making it difficult to move. The sun shined in a large south-facing window. Covered with condensation from so many people breathing warm air against the cold panes, the light appeared bright yellow. I couldn't find a place to sit in the front room. So when I got my coffee and snack I stepped up into a back room that looked like a screened porch in warmer weather. But it too had translucent glass windows covered with condensation. Luckily, I arrive as three people got up from a long picnic table, and I took a seat at the end. A Canadian couple from British Columbia took two seats next to me. After exchanging the usual information, we talked about the day's walk and the anticipation of reaching Santiago in just two days.

I got up and stretched. Wishing the Canadians "buen camino," I left the camaraderie of Café Esperon and got back to the Camino a few meters downhill to the left. The route followed narrow winding streets barely wide enough for a passing car.

Most of the route from here went downhill to Padron. It promised to be difficult for my back, as well as my knees and feet. There were some pretty steep grades along the way, and they put unusual strain on my ankles, quads, and lower back. At some point, I started leaning to the right which would throw me off-balance. I tried to compensate with my walking poles to no avail. Often they even made it worse. At times, I felt helpless to prevent myself from careening to the right, and I was thankful that there were no steep drop-offs. However, several times I almost fell into shallow run-off ditches on the side of the road. The nearer I got to Padron the more painful every step became. The left side of my back hurt as if from a muscle strain, and as I compensated for it, my lower back began to hurt, and my right side started hurting too.

More and more people would ask me if I felt all right or needed help as they passed me. At one point a fellow, leaning to the right, passed as he engaged two other pilgrims in conversation. He didn't look pained, but I knew that he must be hurting.

Before, getting to Padron, I needed to navigate the hilly streets of Pontecesures, a town several kilometers south and on the opposite side of the Rio Ulla from my destination. The wide, brownish-green Rio Ulla moved slowly at this point around a giant smoke belching factory. I followed narrow streets along a ridge high above the river opposite the factory. The residential streets opened occasionally at parks that provided a "scenic" view and often a wall or bench where I could rest.

It seemed as though my stopping became more and more frequent now. It was frustrating to be so close, two or three kilometers, to the end of my day's walk and needing to keep stopping. It got harder to cheer myself on.

Instead, I started cursing my situation, imploring whatever spirits drove me on to be done with the walk.

Just before reaching the bridge over the river, I stopped at a bench on a corner in the shade of a two-story building. At that point, if a bus stopped there, I might have hopped on it. I couldn't wait for the day to be over, and it buoyed my spirits to know that it soon would be.

I pulled myself up wincing, and stepped out into the sun. As I crossed the long span, the sun beat down in blistering heat. "*It was October for Pete's sake,*" I moaned.

On the other side, a few trees and a wall made a suitable place to sit, gather my thoughts once more, and look at the map. My hotel was another kilometer or two up the river and that realization dashed my optimism. "*Damn it,*" I cursed to myself. "*There's still more to walk. Is this ever going to end?*"

The route crossed a roundabout and headed down some residential streets until it passed some fields. When the road came to a canal and a path along it, a yellow arrow pointed to the right and north. Looking ahead, I didn't see any shade for quite some distance. My throat was parched and my feet shuffled along as I tilted to the right. I must have been some sight – kind of like a rabid dog foaming at the mouth and stumbling into a farmyard.

I walked into a long plaza with the town market to my left and a street lined with restaurants to my right. They all appeared busy with lunch time crowds. At the north end of the plaza, I stopped into the Restaurante Mundos to ask for directions. They had prominently displayed their menu del dia at the entrance. As I entered, I noticed a welcome change in the temperature. It was 2 p.m., and with my hotel just two blocks away, I decided to sit down and eat.

I first asked for water, and then realizing that I could get a shower and a nap at my hotel just around the corner, I allowed myself a glass of cold white wine...and then another. The alcohol went right to my head, and my body started to relax and unwind. I couldn't believe that I had made it this far today. I felt good about it. I had made it to Padron.

Thoughts filled with doubt weighed heavily on my mind. I labored over the question whether I could walk all the way to Santiago, a taxing 24 kilometer walk even under good circumstances. At this point I wasn't going to quit. I could rest in Padron the next day, but if I rested before continuing, I didn't know whether the hotel in Santiago would hold my reservation.

Originally I planned to take a bus 11 kilometers to the base of a 7 kilometer climb. That would make my walk to Santiago only 14 kilometers. However, during my walks the past few days since Pontevedra, I had thought a lot about changing my plan. I hadn't resolved the issue yet. Up until this day, I still had hopes of walking the last 14 kilometers.

However, an upcoming event would clinch the decision for me.

24 LAST CAMINO DINNER WITH NEW-FOUND FRIENDS

As I shuffled up to the Hotel Chef Rivera two blocks from the lunch place, the Four Amigos, still dressed in their hiking clothes, sat enjoying cold beverages. They warmly greeted me and asked me to join them. I begged off, promising to return as soon as I checked in.

I was once again thankful for the elevator that took me and my backpack to my third floor room. I splashed water on my face as I painfully bent over the sink. I then bent down to remove my sneakers and put on my sandals. Now, I could be sociable.

I returned downstairs and sat at a table with the four of them and discussed the walk of the past few days. The Four Amigos were not the usual pilgrims. Two of them had walked the Camino Frances several years before. They understood that walking a Camino didn't need to be about deprivation. If you planned properly, it could be enjoyable.

When I went to check in, I noticed large suitcases, the kind you'd need to check on an airplane, were waiting for them like my backpack. They didn't bring backpacks. The larger suitcase format and easier access enabled them to bring more clothes and other things. Most pilgrims, carrying minimum weight in a backpack, would think this luxurious. The large suitcases also explained why they always seemed to be better dressed on the trail than the average pilgrim.

As we sat and traded stories about our walks, I learned that our paths had been similar. They had taken rest days in Baiona and Pontevedra just like me. However, I hadn't seen them in either place. They had stayed in paradors, upscale hotels run by the Spanish government. The cost of a room in a parador costs three to four times what I had been paying. In addition, the paradors in Baiona and Pontevedra were in different parts of the cities than my hotels.

When I met the Amigos in Viladesuso, they had told me that they were combining their walk with a gourmet tour of Galicia. So, at every town where they stayed, they sought out the best restaurants. Our conversation wandered to the food we had tasted, and the restaurant in Caldas that I thought I would return to, but didn't. I told them about the fun night at Hotel Sena where I had stayed to eat dinner. While according to them, I missed an excellent meal, I had had a wonderful evening to remember.

Our plan had been to go to dinner together in Padron. Separately, we had decided to stay at Hotel Chef Rivera. It had a good reputation. Tony had done a little research, and thought we could do better. Besides, on this Thursday, the Chef Rivera dining room looked empty, aged, and uninspiring. We decided to meet for drinks before heading out to another place.

I headed upstairs for the next order of business, a shower and nap. As I stood in the shower washing the day's dirt and sweat off my body, the hot water loosened my muscles, and I became aware that every move hurt me on the left side. I turned facing away from the shower so the stream of water could flow over my back. My back had become so sensitive that the stream hurt where it touched me. I reached around probing the pain. It went from my shoulder blades down to the curve of my back above my hips. I must have had a sprained muscle. This was not good.

"*What have I done?*" I asked myself.

My mind returned to thoughts of walking to Santiago the next day. I wondered whether I could make it…even a shortened 14 kilometer walk. At this point, I didn't think I could, and if I did try to walk it, I might do worse damage to myself.

As I lay on top of the sheets, with the curtains drawn and the air conditioner whirring under the window, I contemplated the few options I had. I was disappointed, and my thoughts went back to the trail between Baiona and Vigo, wishing I had stayed on the bicycle route. The truth is that my legs managed the walk better than I had expected, and if it hadn't been for straining my back, my Camino would have been relatively pain-free.

Before dozing off, I made up my mind. I would take a bus to the other side of the 7 kilometer hill, and then hike the last several kilometers to the cathedral in Santiago. This would cut about 20 kilometers off a 24 kilometer walk, but still enable me to walk into Santiago with other pilgrims. Feeling pretty good about that plan, I drifted off to sleep.

When I went downstairs around 7, an unexpected surprise greeted me. The three women I had had dinner with the night before in Caldas were sitting at a table, having a drink, and talking with the Four Amigos. The women were doing laundry at a self-service laundromat across the street from the hotel and were passing time while washing their clothes. I sat down, and they asked me how I was doing. At this point I unveiled my plan for the next day to the group. Everybody expressed regrets but thought I had devised a reasonable plan.

Judy of the Four Amigos explained that their plans had changed too. Originally they were planning to walk the 24 kilometers to Santiago on the next day, but they were ahead of schedule and the hotel in Santiago didn't have a room for them until the next night. So, they decided to walk an easy 7 kilometers to a town called Escravitude and push on to Santiago the following day, Saturday.

We left the women who had retreated to the laundromat to get their things, and went in search of the restaurant. As we walked away, I realized that I hadn't said goodbye. It didn't matter, I rationalized. I'd never see them again. Nevertheless, I started to understand the fleeting nature of "friendships" on the Camino. You become friends because of common experiences and needs, and when they are over, the friendships fade further and further away as what brought you together also fades in importance.

The Amigos and I went looking for another restaurant Tony had found on Google. We walked north past a plaza. It had become dark while we socialized, and had a difficult time finding the restaurant -- even on the main street. The place had started to close for the night and was almost empty. So we retraced our steps and then crossed the main street. Walking down a narrow street with shops, cafes and restaurants to an alley, we found another restaurant on Tony's list, O Alpendre. When we got there, there were no seats, but the waiter asked us to wait a few minutes until some customers left. He put two tables together right outside the door, and under an awning.

We ordered a bottle of wine, while we looked over the menu and the posted specials. We were a group looking for a big meal and we ordered as if we were an army platoon that just came off of a forced march. We started our order with Padron peppers. How could you have a dinner in Padron without Padron peppers? Then there were *Chiperones*, which in Galicia is squid. We ordered it grilled and fried. Next we ordered *bacalao* which is dried, salted cod prepared Galician style, baked in a tomato sauce. There was also mussels al vapor, steamed in white wine. And finally little clams, *almejas*, in tiny round shells. I'm not sure whether we ordered fried anchovies, but we probably did.

When you travel alone, you can't eat like this. When

you're in a group you can share. This dinner brought me back to the first lunch I had in A Guarda where I sat and watched groups of tourists feast on plates of seafood. I had only been in Spain a little over a week, but it seemed like such a long time ago. I remember reading forums about the seafood in Galicia, and particularly one pilgrim who never really understood how to order a meal until, after he finished his Camino, and went to dinner with a group of Spanish friends. Like my dinner this evening, he sat with his friends in front of platters filled with delectable foods, much of which he had never tasted.

While we sat and drank the first bottle of wine, we got to know each other better. We talked about why we were walking the Camino and our backgrounds. I told them about my hip replacement, my retirement in Mexico, and my background in marketing. When the subject of wine came up, they were interested in my experiences owning a winery.

Bob and Tony had been friends for many years, and had met working for a large media company. Tony went on to run a spin-off company with a name that anyone growing up with cable TV would recognize. Bob went into designing and publishing specialty books, built an international company, and had recently sold it. The conversation became wide-ranging.

Maybe my Camino was ending too soon, I thought. I had started alone, talking with very few people about anything of substance. In the past several days, the evenings had become very social, with interesting conversations about a wide variety of subjects. If I were only 12 days into the

Camino Frances, would the next 40 days of walking be as sociable? I'll never find out.

When the topic of "would you do another Camino" came up, I didn't hesitate. "No way! Been there, done that," I answered.

I'm not sure why people walk multiple Caminos. The Amigos were doing the Camino Portugues, because it passed through a part of the world they hadn't known, and what better way to discover it than on-foot.

Maybe, if I were 30 years younger, I'd do another Camino. But there's a lot of world to see, and not much time to see it. I don't want to spend all my travel time hiking in Spain. South America beckoned me again, and I wanted to visit Southeast Asia while I still could. And, I had barely scratched the surface of Mexico where I live, an incredibly beautiful country with diverse cultures, fantastic food, and amazing history.

When our food arrived, we could hardly find room on the table for it all. The mussels were plump and sweet. The chiperone was sweeter. The bacalao surprised us all, baked in a delicious savory tomato sauce and the fish still sweet and flaky. The peppers still had a slight crunch, and we waded through a generous portion of clams, but not generous enough. I can never get enough of those tasty morsels. We went through three more bottles of wine before we saw a waitress passing several times with a delicious looking dessert. We couldn't resist and placed two orders to share. She brought us a multi-layered cake with chocolate and dulce de leche, which the waitress told us was an old recipe of the owner's grandmother.

At the hotel, we said goodbye and wished each other luck, not knowing if we'd ever see each other again.

25 WALKING INTO SANTIAGO

The next morning, Friday, October 5, after taking a pain killer, I sat on the edge of the bed and performed my pre-walk ritual. I had done it almost every day for the past three months, and every morning of my Camino, except in Pontevedra. It felt different this morning. It would be the last time I needed to do it for a while. After I finished my Camino, I'd be traveling all over Spain for a month with my girlfriend. Oh, I'd be walking, but not like I had been. There would be little need for taping my heels, and wearing an ankle brace.

I had mixed feelings as I grunted while bending over to lace my sneakers. On the one hand, I felt a little sad, and at the same time exhilarated that my Camino experience would be ending in a few hours. I'd be at the steps of the cathedral in Santiago, and it would suddenly be over. I knew people, the three women I met in Caldas for example, who would be continuing on a few more days to the Atlantic Ocean at Fisterra or Muxia. But, for most of us pilgrims, the Camino would end in Santiago.

I'm not Catholic, so the cathedral, itself, held no deep meaning for me. It had been the goal post that I pushed a ball toward every day. With my sneakers laced, I sat in Padron, ready to kick for the goal.

I always felt a little conflicted referring to myself as a pilgrim because I really wasn't -- at least not a religious pilgrim. I was a walker or trekker who followed the pilgrim route. At times, as I walked among others with more serious purpose, I felt like an imposter, sort of like the faux marathon runner who never wears a number. He can run the race, but he'll never win a medal. I didn't need a medal, but I wanted one. I had a credencial, but I could have been satisfied with the very act of completing a walk of 100 miles. I could have walked 100 miles anywhere, but the Camino was the reason I did.

If it weren't for the wonder drug, ibuprofen, I wouldn't have made it this far, or gotten a restful night's sleep in days. I took my backpack to the lobby, and asked the clerk about busses to Santiago. The day before, I had found the bus station on Google Maps, but I wanted to make sure I didn't miss a bus and have to wait hours for the next one. She thought there would be one around 9 and another at 10. I decided to check.

The station lay several long blocks to the north just off the main street. As I started walking there, before eight, I relished another beautiful cloudless day. It dawned on me that I had not experienced any rain since arriving in Porto. Except for a few foggy mornings along the coast, there had hardly been a cloud. I had heard stories of people who had walked through rain and snow to get to Santiago, and I considered myself incredibly lucky.

As I turned the corner outside the hotel, I noticed a busy-looking café. It stood there, like so many I'd seen on this trip, Café Bar Galicia, and made a mental note to come back if I had time.

"*It's almost over*," I told myself as I started walking. "*It's almost over.*"

I've done a bit of extensive travel where I've moved from place to place many times over the course of weeks or months. This emotion is nothing new. There comes a time, in my travels when I start to grow weary of constantly moving, and long to go home, or to just stay put for a while. Good or bad, I've found that the closer I get to the end of a long trip, the stronger these feelings get.

So, after a block, my morning stiffness began to disappear and I walked with a spring in my step. Just past the center of town and the plaza where I had been wandering around with the Amigos in search of a restaurant, the street became the usual clutter of auto parts stores, little groceries, abandoned storefronts, closed restaurants, and an occasional vacant lot. The bus station occupied a cream-colored building set back from the other side of the main street. The ticket office sat next to a small café that barely looked open. I checked the schedule posted on the wall and noted 9:15 and 10:00 am trips to Santiago. The clock said: 8:00. I had plenty of time to get breakfast. Rather than going into the depressing looking station café, I returned to Café Bar Galicia.

As I approached the café door, a small man approached me. Ever since Redondela, we had been passing each other. I would take a break and he would pass me. Then he would take a break and I would pass him. After a while, we politely greeted each other and nodded our heads as we passed. We had never talked. This diminutive looking man couldn't have been more than 5'6" tall, had a well-trimmed gray beard that went from ear to ear and wrapped around his chin. If he had a little fedora on his head, he could have been mistaken for a munchkin or maybe one of Santa's helpers.

As he approached, he seemed to be disturbed about something. He anxiously explained that he wanted to get a taxi to Santiago, but no one would take him. He wanted to know if he could find one, whether I'd be willing to share the ride and fare with him. I said that I would, but then asked him why he wanted to take a cab when he could take a bus leaving in about an hour. I explained that I had just been to the bus station, and that, for just a few Euros, we could take a bus. He retreated to think about it.

Meanwhile, I ordered a coffee and croissant, and then had my credencial stamped for the last time. As I sat down at a table, the elfish man came up holding a cup of coffee and asked if he could join me. I said yes, of course, but I really had no interest in talking, or finding a travel companion. This was an important day, and I would have preferred to experience it alone, as I had the first day of my Camino.

The man spoke with a French accent and claimed he didn't know much English. We sat across from each other and talked as best we could. His proficiency in English eclipsed my knowledge of French. He approved of taking the bus. I assured him the station wasn't very far and we had plenty of time.

My new travel partner's name was Maurice. He was French, and seventy-five, four years older than me. This was his third Camino. We talked about why we weren't walking all the way to Santiago. He had been walking from Porto, and had had enough. After all, he had walked into Santiago before on previous Caminos. In retrospect, I think he had another reason, because as soon as we reached the cathedral, he took off claiming that he needed to be somewhere.

We walked together to the bus station and arrived a little early. We waited separately. I wanted to sit down, but couldn't stop pacing. When the bus arrived, I hobbled up the steps and paid the driver about 2 Euros for a ticket. Maurice followed me, and took a seat across the aisle. As the bus pulled out of the station, I leaned into the aisle so I could see the road ahead.

The Camino route followed the highway for a while. Civilization had grown over what may have been a bucolic rural setting at one time. The results of unregulated urban sprawl littered the highway, intermittently industrial, commercial, and residential. Backpack-clad pilgrims were streaming out of Padron and lined the highway, hiking on shoulders, sidewalks, and through parking lots. In one sense, I wanted to be walking with them. In another, I was glad I wasn't.

The road climbed the 7 kilometer hill and through

Milladoiro, a suburb where tall apartment buildings line the highway. After passing through the town, the twin spires of the cathedral became visible in the distance. For many, after walking fifty days, the first view of the cathedral is an inspiring moment. Seeing it through the bus's windshield motivated me to continue my Camino as soon as the bus could safely let me off. Walking from here appeared feasible. I was close enough now. I could taste the finish.

The bus navigated several roundabouts and turn-offs before heading down the hill to the Sar River. When the bus drove over the river, I saw a person walking with a back pack, and pointed it out to Maurice. I told him that I was getting off at the next stop. I got up from my seat, and walked up to the driver. Maurice followed, and within 10 seconds we were on the sidewalk looking for a yellow arrow.

We were on Rua da Volta do Castro. The street rose gradually from the river. The walk from here to the Cathedral would be an uphill climb. How fitting! Maurice and I walked side by side. He walked almost as slow as me. Two and three story apartment buildings lined the street, many of which had storefronts on the ground level. We didn't speak much, collecting our thoughts, except at street corners where we'd look for a yellow arrow to guide us to the next street corner. My excitement continued to build with the anticipation of finishing. I felt an edgy impatience as the street seemed to go on forever. Maybe the next street would lead to the cathedral - or the next. We passed through several roundabouts, and crossed at numerous traffic lights. The route kept going uphill.

Maurice and I walked on without stopping or resting. At this point, our single-purpose and *raison d' etre* impelled us to get to the cathedral. Rua da Volta do Castro became Avenida da Xoan Carlos I. On and on we walked until we were walking along the red-brick wall of the Parque de Alameda. The park seemed much greener and better kept than the park of the same name in A Guarda where I started my walk only twelve days before.

26 THE COMPOSTELA

After crossing a busy intersection at the end of the wall, we found ourselves in the historic district looking ahead at a maze of walking streets.

Even though Maurice had been here before, he couldn't figure out which way to go. So, I approached a middle aged woman dressed in black, and asked her how to get to the cathedral. She could see we were pilgrims, and without hesitation said "follow me" and motioned with her hand. She walked at a fast clip, and if I had walked the entire route from Padron, I don't think I could have kept up with her. She started down one of the streets that spoked off of the intersection, Rua do Franco, and quickly angled to the right down Rua do Vilar.

The street, lined with shops and restaurants, bustled with late morning foot traffic. She weaved between tourists, shop owners, and waiters carrying trays of food to outside tables. She deftly led us in an out of the cool shade of a covered walkway on the left side, and into the center of the street. I had all I could do to keep from bumping into people and tripping over my own feet. I held my walking poles close to my body so I wouldn't hurt passersby. After what seemed like a long walk, she started to slow down as the street opened into the Praza das Praterias, more like a courtyard than a plaza. Straight ahead at the top of a large, wide stairway, I saw a side entrance to the cathedral with a line of tourists and pilgrims waiting their turns to enter.

Maurice and I thanked her. She turned and walked back into the maze of streets. Maurice and I shook hands, hugged and wished each other well. And then, claiming he needed to be somewhere, he disappeared into the crowd downhill toward the front of the cathedral.

Then, I heard someone call my name. I looked around searching for the source. "Up here, John," the voice yelled once more. I looked up to see Ernst, the Bavarian, I had shared a bunk bed with in Redondela. He had parted with the harem, and waited on line to see the cathedral. I waved to him from below and limped my way to the top of the stairs. We shook hands and hugged, congratulating each other on our achievements. He had arrived the day before and would be heading to Fisterra by bus later in the day. It's hard to say how I felt when Ernst and I said goodbye. I had a hollow feeling inside. Ironically, I needed to walk a little and absorb the moment before my next task.

In retrospect, I've concluded that friendships on a Camino aren't really friendships. They are, at best acquaintances. You "happen" into relationships while you are on your pilgrimage, and then you consciously "destroy" them at the end, returning, changed in important ways, to whatever life you had before. They remind me of an experience my ex-wife once described to me. She was in a college art class about the *process* of creating and learning things along the way; not the final product. At the end of the course, the professor made everyone destroy their semester-long portfolios of class projects. It was a difficult thing to do, but it had an important lesson about life.

I had made it to Santiago. The long walk was over. Step by step I had walked from A Guarda. I never thought I could do it. Yet I knew I would.

A purist would say that I cheated in getting there. Yes, I skipped 5 kilometers between Baiona and Vigo, and 5 kilometers the next day between Vigo and Redondela, and 20 kilometers on my final day. I had walked 130 out of the 160 I planned, but I never felt that I had cheated. When I got hurt, I hadn't turned back. I had adjusted to accommodate my needs.

I imagine, before cars, busses and trains, it was more difficult to quit. You might as well walk forward to Santiago as back to your home. To make the walk, it had to be a calling. You were leaving your family for months at a time. Today's modern world imposes time constraints, forcing us to jam a pilgrimage into so many days before returning to everyday life. To some, a pilgrimage may still be a calling, but in many ways it is easier to fulfill.

Before getting a cup of coffee, I wanted to find the Camino office. The Camino is a big business. In 2018, almost 400,000 people officially walked a Camino, and the number has consistently gone up every year. There is a small bureaucracy, augmented by volunteers from around the world that manage the activities related to it and collect money to help maintain it. It occupies a building downhill from the cathedral. For many, like me, it's the first stop after getting to the city.

I hadn't gone to my hotel yet. I couldn't check-in until 1, and it was only 11. Descending the steps from where I had found Ernst on line, I turned right to go around the Cathedral to the Praza do Obradoiro, a massive stone plaza separating the cathedral and the city hall. I asked two policemen how to get to the Camino office. They pointed to a walkway on the other side of the plaza that led down an incline. I walked with a purpose and surveyed the activity on the Plaza as I walked.

I gazed up at the cathedral and the activity on the plaza. As cathedrals go, from the outside, it wasn't the most impressive that I had seen. It belied, I would find out, the magnificence of the silver and gold treasures inside. Even though the building dominated the space, presenting a majestic façade for the plaza, the true wonder took place in front of it.

People from all over the world, speaking numerous languages gathered there sharing and relishing a few moments of triumph. The months of planning and training, the weeks or months of slogging through every day, in all kinds of weather, for hundreds of kilometers, had come to a sudden stop when they reached the Plaza in front of the cathedral.

I believe an incredible sense of accomplishment, as well as a sense of disbelief must have overwhelmed most of them. Some were in tears. They were milling around saying good bye to fellow pilgrims, or sprawled out on the pavement staring up at the twin spires. At any point in time, hundreds of them might be coming and going. They walked from France or Portugal or from other places in Spain and other starting points all over Europe.

The Pilgrim office reinforced the international nature of the Camino. As I entered the modern antiseptic building, a person handed me a form to fill-out and ushered me down a hallway to the end of a long line. As I passed, people were speaking a potpourri of languages in hushed tones. A charged excitement filled the hallways as people patiently waited to present their credentials at the office. You could feel the sense of relief in the way people would begin to relax shortly after getting on line.

The office, itself reminded me of the motor vehicle agency. The morning sunlight streamed in the windows behind a long row of chest-high counters dressed in neutral colors. Before entering, a person sitting at a table asked me whether I had walked the Camino for religious reasons or another reason. The importance of the question became apparent because one of the types of certification or compostela required a fee.

The person directed me to a young lady behind the counter to the far left of the room. She looked at my credencial, asked me where I had started my Camino, and why I had walked it. Since seeing the movie, "The Way," I had actually thought about what I would answer. Without blinking, I looked at her and said:

"I needed to shake up my life."

27 REFLECTING ON MY EXPERIECE

"…I could have missed the pain but I'd have had to miss the dance."

From "The Dance"
Written by Tony Arata
Sung by Garth Brooks

I stood at the desk in the Pilgrim office as the woman filled out a certificate in Latin. She wrote in a calligraphic style with a special black pen. Then she congratulated me as she handed the compostela to me.

I was now officially done! I wanted an anti-climactic yet celebratory cup of coffee!

Turning right outside the building, I walked back behind the town hall until I found steps leading up to the plaza in front of the Cathedral. Along the way there, I found a café on the right, Restaurante Roxoi. Several groups of pilgrims were already having a snack, and a rowdy group of cyclists on the steps were taking pictures with the cathedral behind them between sips of beer.

As I stretched my legs, and sipped my coffee, I started to experience feelings I never could have anticipated during those long, hot, training sessions during the previous summer. I became kind of numb and needed some time to process what I saw and felt. It would take me several days before I began to understand the importance of the moment and how it affected me.

I planned to stay in Santiago three nights. There were several experiences during that time that helped form my thoughts. On the second day, I took a walk to find the bus station. On the way, I passed the street where several of the Caminos from the east and north enter the city. On that chilly, overcast October morning, I witnessed a steady stream of pilgrims, probably thousands a day, with backpacks and hiking poles walking the sidewalks that meandered through the city leading to the cathedral. A space traveler hovering above the planet, looking at the throngs of people converging on this place, might wonder what was happening there.

I had the second experience while attending the Pilgrims Mass. More than the mass itself, the people interested me. I looked at them, old and young, couples and singles, knowing what they had gone through to get there. Everyone in the church shared a unique experience that is difficult to explain in any other terms than spiritual.

For the people who walked for religious reasons, being at this very special place for Catholics, must have had a significance that we non-Catholics can't understand. Along the way, as I walked, I met people who were trying to find a meaning in their life, get over a loss, take a vacation, or take on a new challenge.

Even though the cathedral where I sat had been the destination I set out to reach, my Camino had become more than the destination. Risking a cliché, it started to become clearer that my Camino was about the journey I had taken.

When I walked in the trenches, so to speak, I didn't reflect very much about what I was doing. In a sad way, every day had been a grunt to get from point A to point B. I met people from all over every day, walked and talked with them for a kilometer or two. I saw people helping each other, and there were some who helped me. You knew that almost everyone fought some pain - blisters, ankles, arches, backs, knees, shin splints, shoulders, bladders, etc. - but no one showed it. They pressed on, grateful for the occasional cafe where they could rest for a while. Even though you might not know anyone, you could sense camaraderie amongst everyone.

I think the camaraderie made my Camino special. I was walking alone...but I wasn't.

***

Finally, when I decided to walk, I never intended to write a book about it. I didn't take copious notes, photos, or videos. There is no way a photo could convey my inner experiences, thoughts and reflections. I only planned to share my journey via emails with a small list of interested friends. The experiences I could convey in those emails were too limited because of time and technology constraints. Because of that, I felt compelled to share more in this book.

In retrospect, I wish I had done a better job of chronicling my adventures while they were fresh in my mind. I regret that I can't remember the names of many of the people I met. Where significant, I gave them names. And where I remembered them, I often changed them.

I wish I had taken more pictures of the countryside, food, and the menus. However, in many cases, modern technology helped to refresh my memory, and I will discuss its role in the next chapter. I was amazed at how much of the Camino route was visible on Google Street View, even some dirt roads through the woods. Restaurant listings with tempting photos reminded me of many of the meals I enjoyed.

Since returning from Spain, and in preparation for writing this book, I researched what others have written, especially those of a similar age. Even for someone who isn't Catholic or even religious, the Camino experience can be very moving. That said, some will be critical of the way I did my Camino. There are purists who claim that the only true way to experience a Camino is as they imagine pilgrims of another era did it – walking it in its entirety, not taking shortcuts, carrying all your needs on your back, staying in humble accommodations, and more. Some say that a Camino experience should involve suffering and sacrifice. As I learned, no one walks it without sacrifice or escapes physical, and sometimes, emotional pain.

Regardless, I am not a purist. Everyone's Camino

experiences are different, and I refuse to be judgmental about anyone that undertakes such a monumental task -- even those who are unable to finish. As far as I'm concerned, there is no right or wrong way to do it. At the very least, walking 100 kilometers or more to Santiago on foot is a significant personal achievement.

28 OBSERVATIONS OF THE MODERN CAMINO

When I first thought about walking the Camino, my vision was of strolling through beautiful woods, lush vineyards, and waving fields of grass and grain. These are the kinds of places that lend themselves to a peaceful and contemplative journey.

However, modernity has impacted the Camino de Santiago at every step. I won't judge whether this is good or bad, but as I learned, today's Camino is not your great grandfathers Camino. Urban growth, electronic technology, cheap airfare, and even rising standards of living, have made the modern Camino more accessible to more people than at any time in history.

Centuries ago, people found their way to Santiago on rustic trails and byways, many of which were replaced long ago with modern thoroughfares. Pilgrims came on foot, on horses and donkeys, on carts, and the rich came by carriage. Today, the Camino welcomes bicyclers and the physically challenged with their own defined routes.

Cities and towns that were once small villages have expanded into sprawling suburbs that have encroached on the ancient way. In many places, the Camino route is shared with modern highways and suburban streets. Once bucolic paths are bordered with ugly factories, large box stores, and their massive parking lots.

The statistics show that the number of people walking the Camino continues to increase every year. It's also not surprising that, as the baby boomer generation reaches retirement age, the number of pilgrims over-sixty is growing as a percentage of all pilgrims. This unbridled growth inevitably puts a strain on the entire system, whether it be the trail system, maintenance of markers, or the support services along the routes. In addition, I've heard complaints from other pilgrims about over-crowding on certain sections of the Camino, especially the 100 kilometer section from Sarria to Santiago.

These changes are a concern of the Church and Pilgrim Office in Santiago. They are exploring ways to preserve the historical traditions and promote the religious nature of the pilgrimage in the face of modern changes. While the 100 kilometer requirement for a compostela only came into being in 1993, there are discussions of either increasing the requirement or doing away with it entirely.

There is little we can do about what happened in the past. Of more concern to me, even as a non-Catholic, is preserving the spiritual and physical beauty of the pilgrimage experience for future generations.

On the positive side, the growth of participation has given rise to new support services, including restaurants, albergues, hotels, as well as other travel services which make a pilgrimage easier and more accessible to a wider variety of people such as me. In addition, some of these services have helped breathe new life into small villages along the route.

There are as many ways to walk the Camino as there are people who do it. A lot of people freelance it. They throw a pack on their back, start hiking, and stop at an albergue whenever they've had enough for the day. Others, like me, plan every detail. And there are others still, like my friend Connie, who used a planning service, like a travel agency, to make all her arrangements. And, there are all sorts of variations in between.

The modern Camino enables pilgrims to plan their experience from an *a la carte* menu of options. Traditionally, pilgrims stayed and ate in albergues. The opportunities for this experience still abound. But, albergues have changed too. I stayed in two private albergues with modern bathroom facilities, mattresses better than my own at home, and semi-private rooms.

However, many albergues don't accept reservations and work on a first-come-first-served basis. During busy seasons, it can be difficult to find accommodations. My friends, Jim and Kathy, after slogging through a cold rain all day couldn't get into an albergue at which they were planning to stay. They needed to walk a few kilometers more before they found an albergue that had room. I'm sure that experience disheartened them. Obviously, pilgrims want to avoid such situations, so they often rise early and stop early…by 2 or 3 pm.

Technology has played a huge role in how one plans for and executes a Camino. Just a few examples include the accessibility of information, the ease of finding accommodations, GPS capabilities, and finding convenience services. It's all there on the Internet.

Many of the guide books that a few years ago were only available in print, are now available electronically. Some have versions that use GPS to locate a pilgrim's position, keep them from getting lost, provide historical background on notable sites, and suggest services en route. Google Maps and its Street View functionality played a significant role in my planning. For the most part, I knew where I was going.

There are also a number of online forums, such as caminosantiago.me, where past and future pilgrims can share information and help each other before and after their pilgrimage.

With more people of means and those over sixty doing pilgrimages, different accommodation options have popped up to cater to an aging clientele and others. A growing number of people are staying at budget hotels that have become easier to find, especially in out-of-the-way places, through online services such as Booking.com or AirBnB.com.

I spent a lot of time on Booking.com, and reserved several months in advance. Consequently, I knew where I would be sleeping every night. There are good points and bad ones for planning like I did. Yes, it removes a certain degree of uncertainty and anxiety about your Camino. Also, if I didn't know where I would be at the end of the day, I would have had to carry my full pack which weighed about 17 pounds. However, such a tight schedule added a rigidity. That meant when I wanted to change my plans, it would have been a logistics nightmare.

For those averse to planning themselves, there are services, such as Camino Ways that act like a Camino tour company. They'll help you plan your route, arrange accommodations, and in some cases, hook you up with a group and provide guides.

I was delighted to find out that there are services that can help you move your pack or suitcases from one place of accommodation to another. At my age and physical condition, I wasn't looking forward to carrying a 17 pound pack 20 kilometers day after day. I used a service called Tuitrans to transport my backpack between hotels. It made walking easier, enabling me to have a more enjoyable pilgrimage. There are other companies that also offer that type of service, including the Spanish Post Office.

All of these changes, in part, have contributed to the recent fast growth of participation because they make undertaking a pilgrimage much more doable. I would anticipate that the Camino will continue to be more accessible which will, in turn, drive up participation. Whether you are a healthy young adult or an aging septuagenarian with joint problems or chronic medical conditions, Santiago is more reachable than ever before.

WALK BY MY SIDE

ABOUT THE AUTHOR

 John Comando is retired and living in Mexico. He loves to travel. In autumn, 2018, he walked the Camino de Santiago in Spain. *Walk by My Side,* a travel memoir, is about that journey and is his first book. He has studied in Spain, adopted children in South America, built houses for Habitat for Humanity, and traveled extensively in Europe and Latin America. For a living John spent 35 years in high-tech marketing, most recently as an independent consultant. Among other things, he ghost wrote dozens of articles bylined by executives that appeared in trade publications in a number of industries. John is also a former winemaker and owned a boutique winery. For fun, John cooks, blogs, writes articles for a local newspaper, as well as short stories and essays, and sings at open mics and karaoke.

You can find more about John at…

WalkCaminoBook.com

RetirednSingleblog.wordpress.com

What Did You Think of
Walk by My Side?

Thank you for purchasing Walk by My Side. I hope you enjoyed it.

I also hope that it fulfilled the promise I stated in the book's description: When I first started writing this book I had a friend read an early chapter where I started walking the Camino. Her comment to me was "I felt like I was walking with you, walking by your side." That comment inspired the book's title and a promise to the reader to maintain that feeling throughout the journey.

If so, it would be really nice if you could share this book with your friends, family, and anyone else with an interest in the subject matter, by posting to **Facebook** *and* **Twitter**.

I'd also greatly appreciate it, if you could take some time to post a review on **Amazon** *and / or* **Good Reads**. *Your feedback and support will help this author to greatly improve his writing craft for future projects and make this book even better.*

Once again, thank you for reading Walk by My Side *and your support.*

John Comando

Printed in Great Britain
by Amazon

34911533R00098